Mandala
Nifty Coloring

Copyright: Published in the United States by Rosanna Cardenas
Published January 2017
ISBN-13: 978-1542651448
ISBN-10: 1542651441

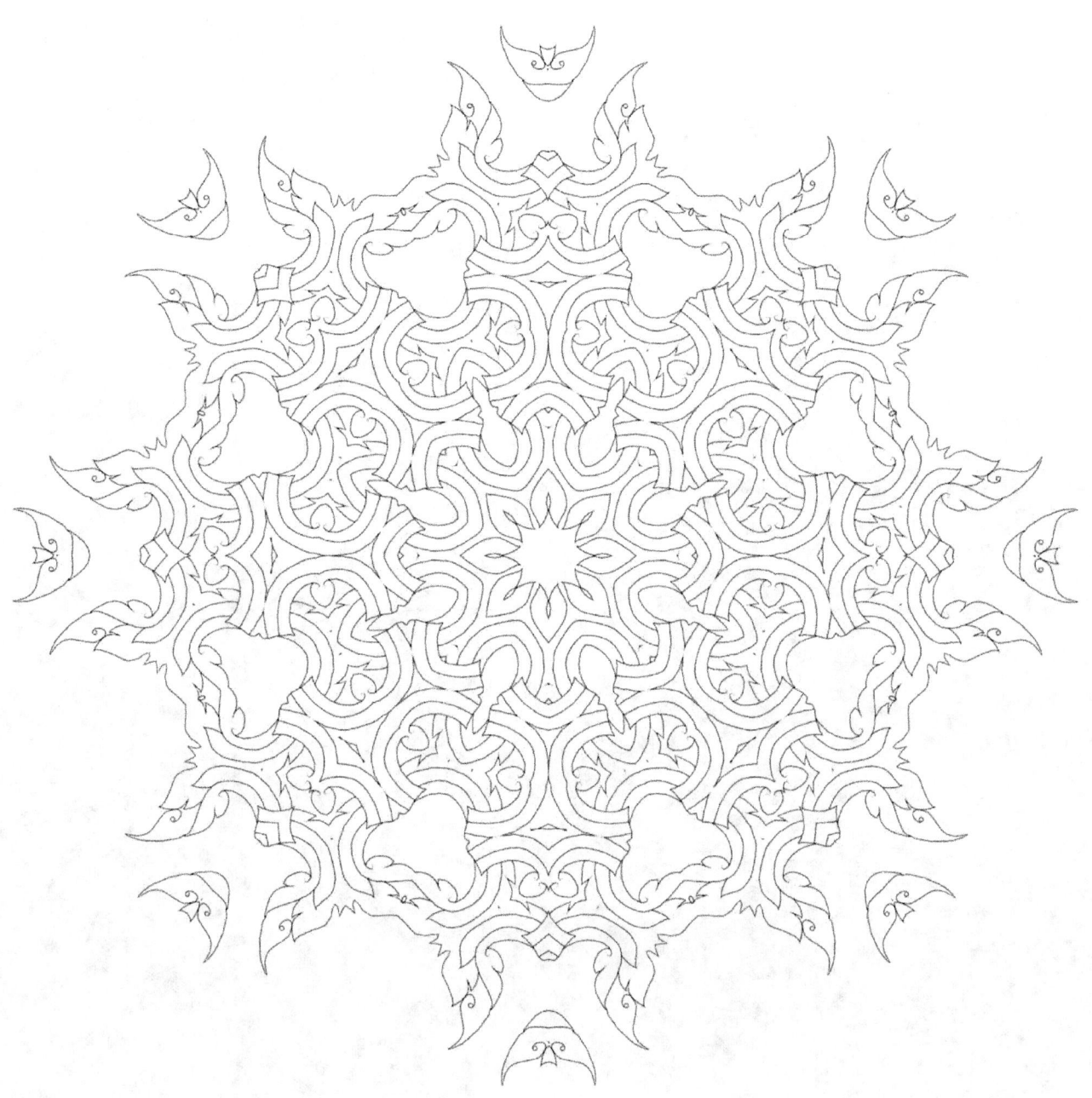

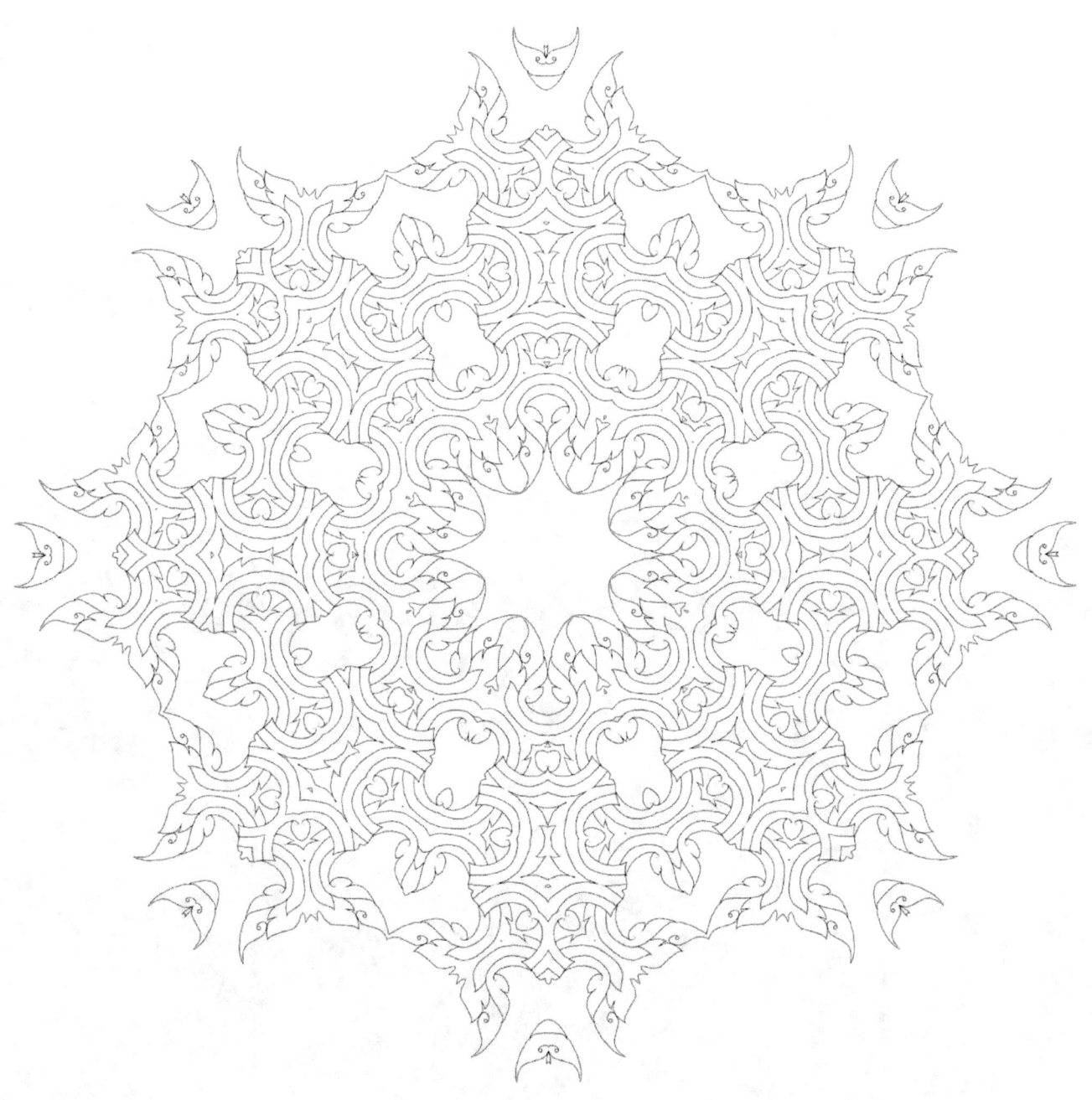

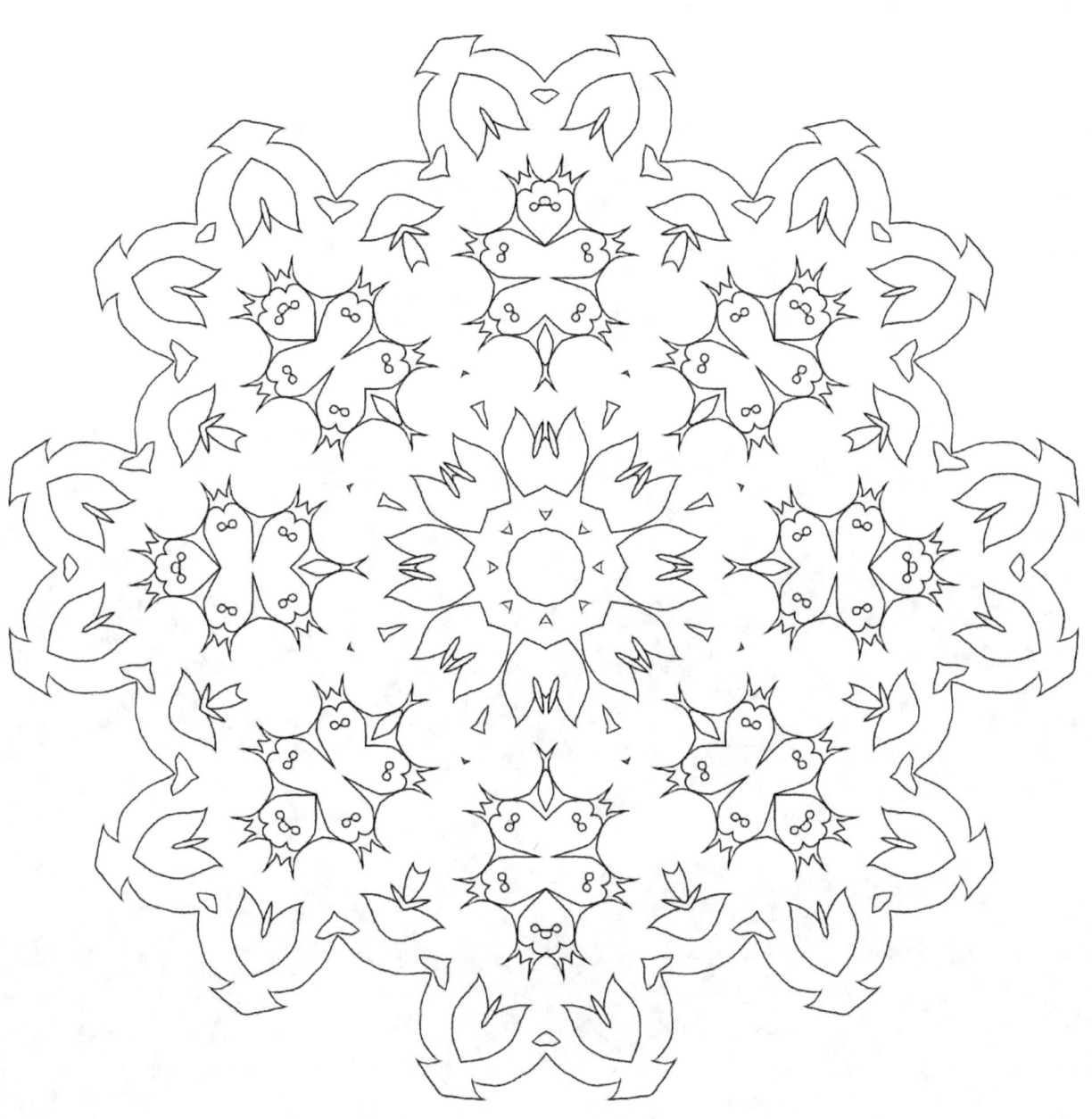

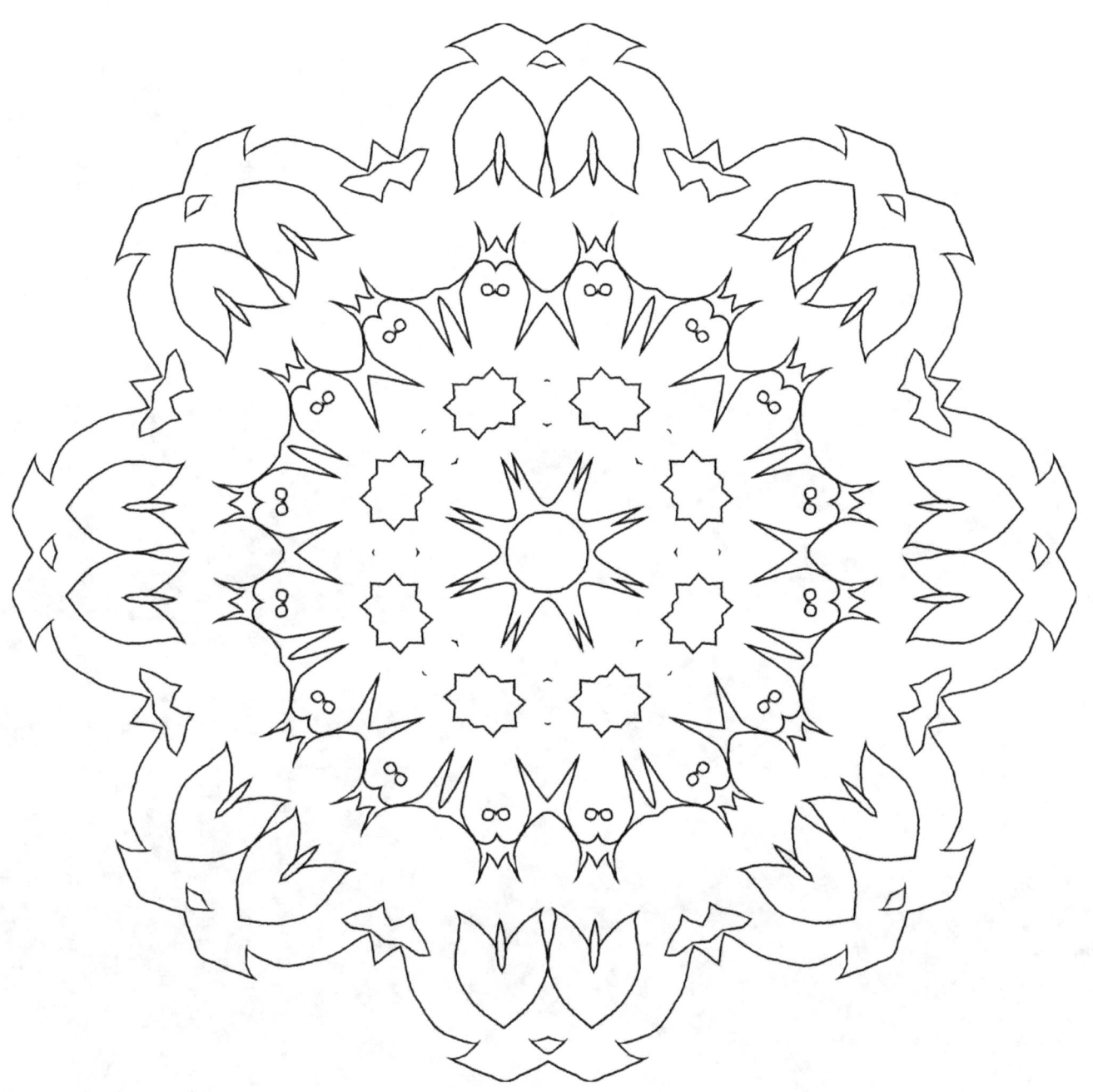

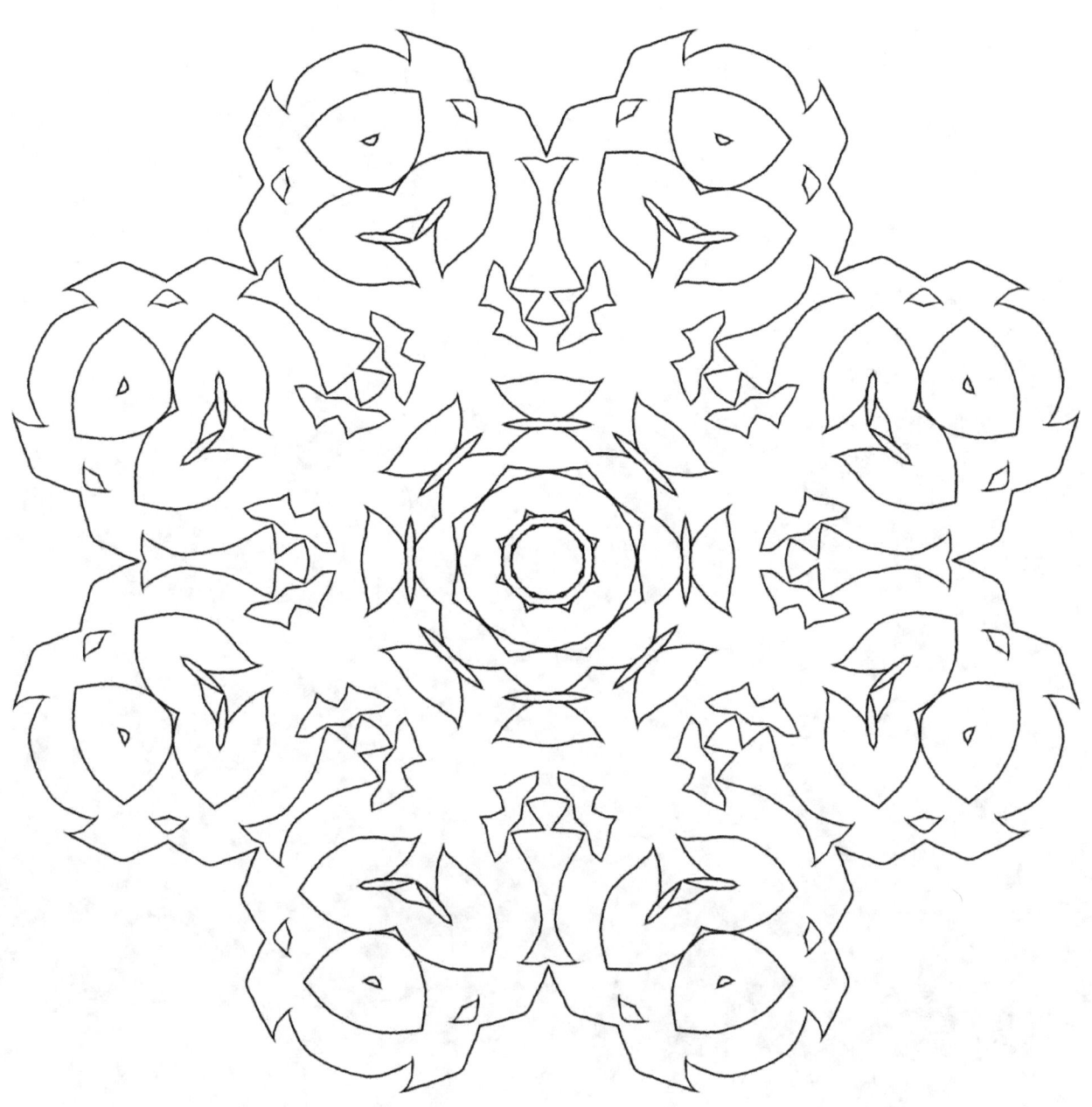

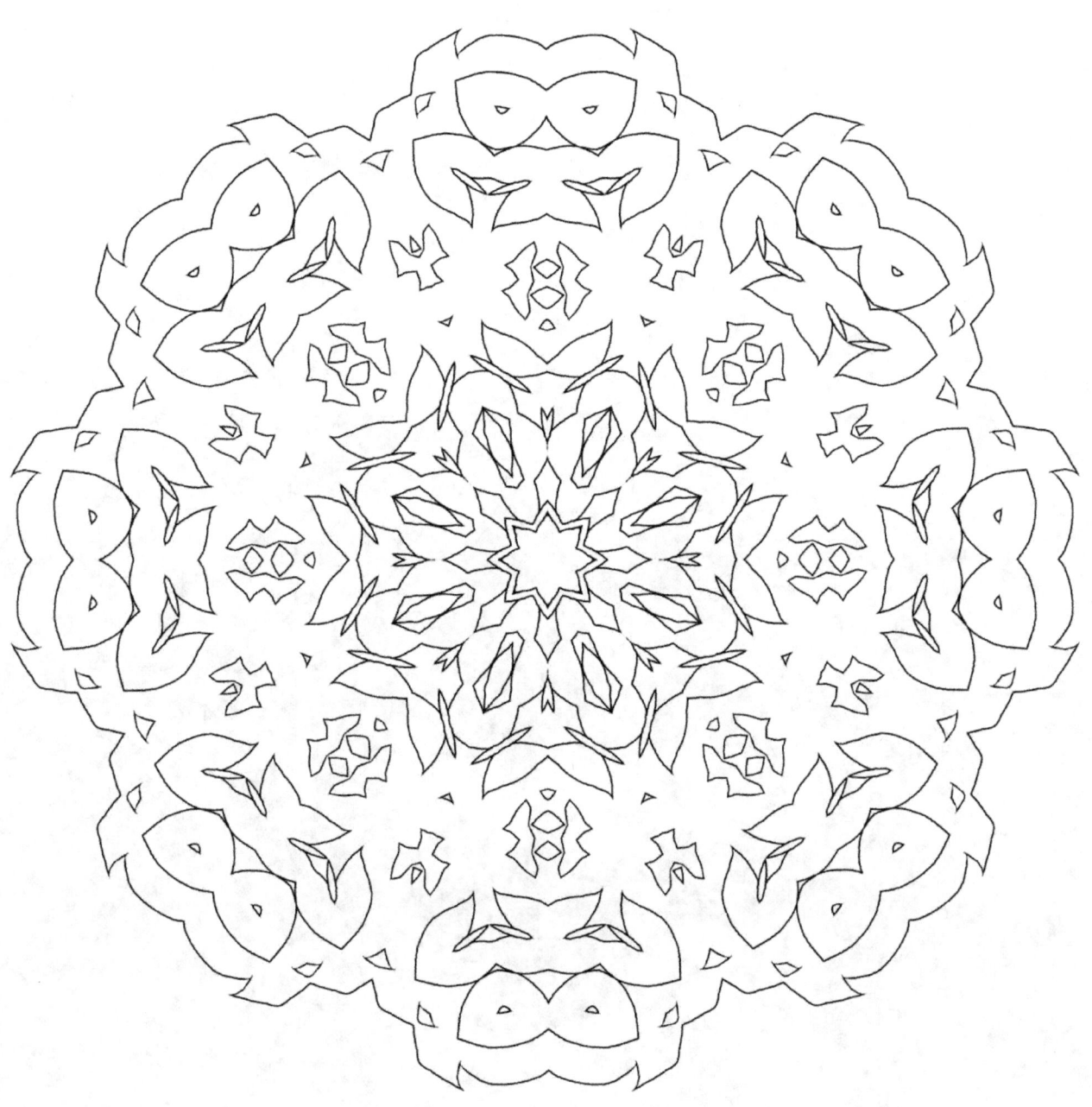

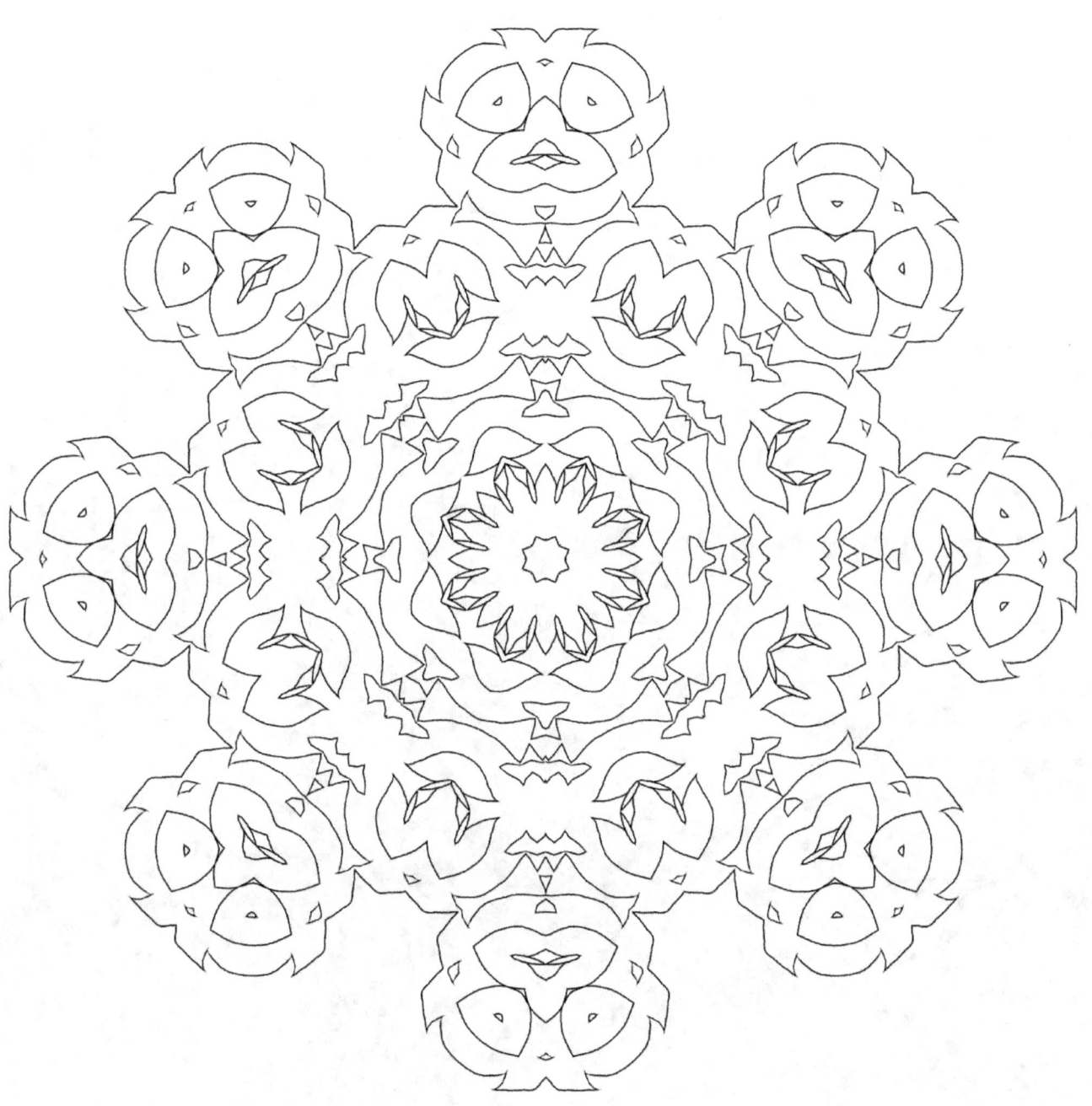

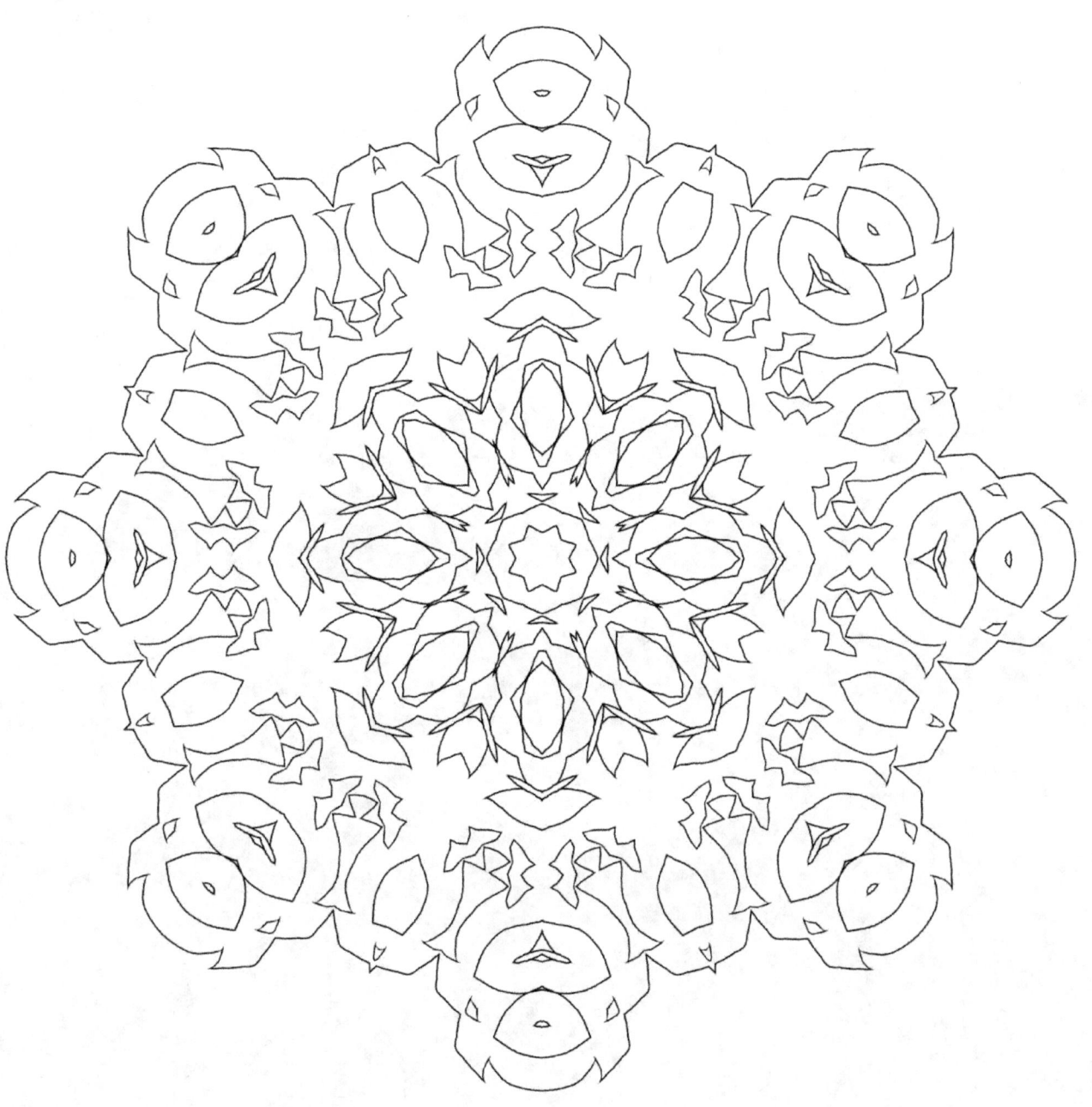

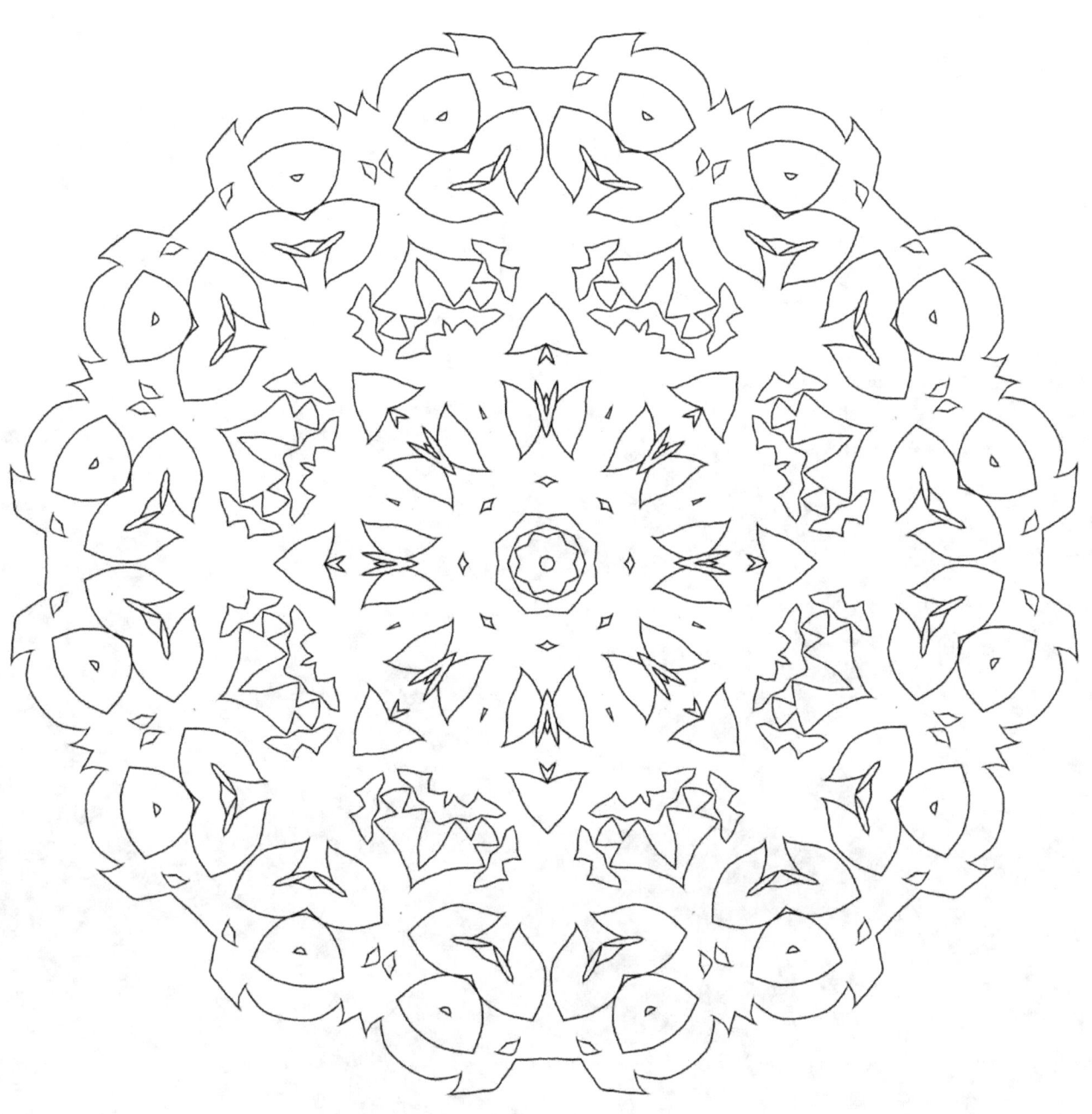

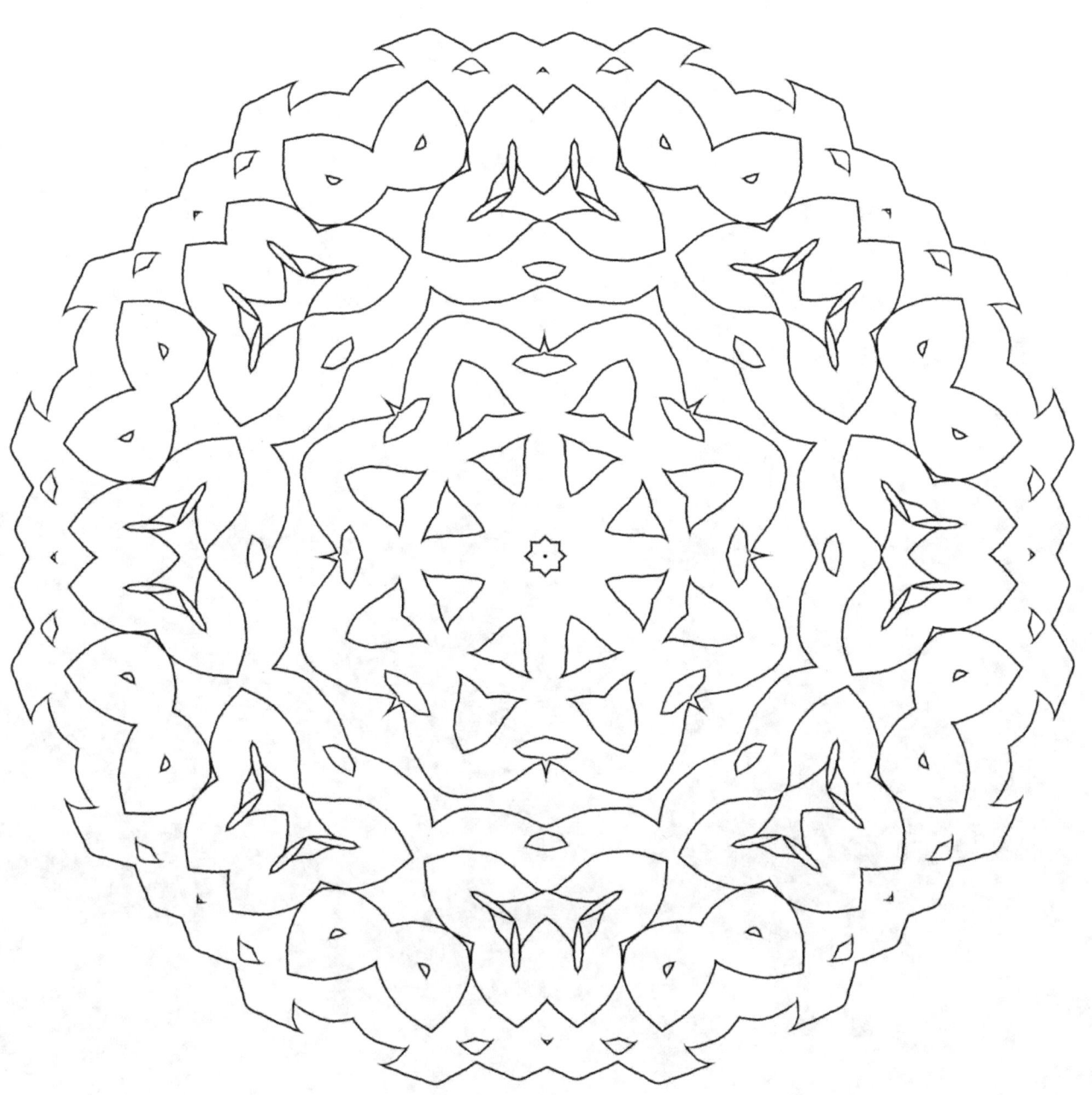

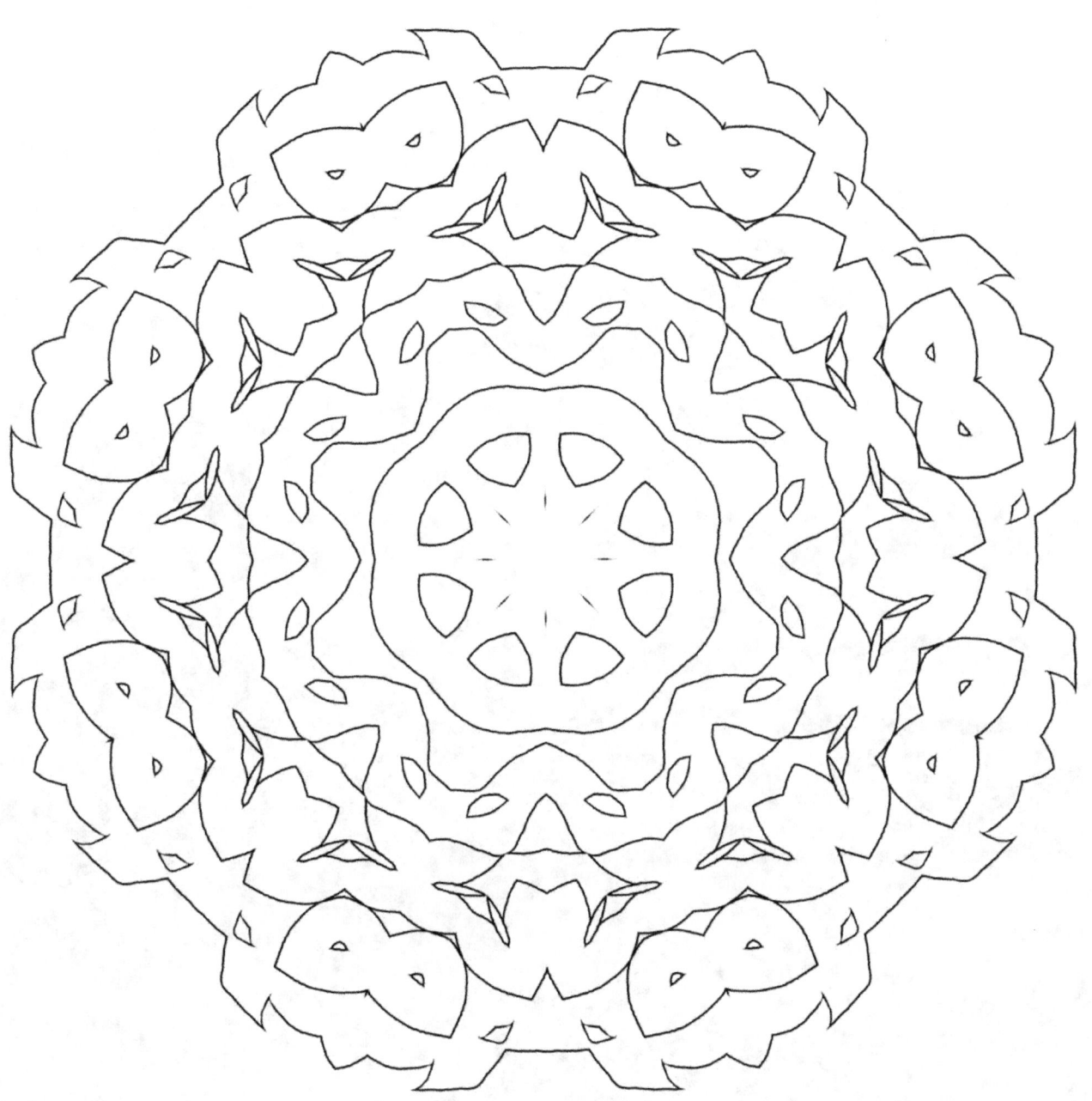

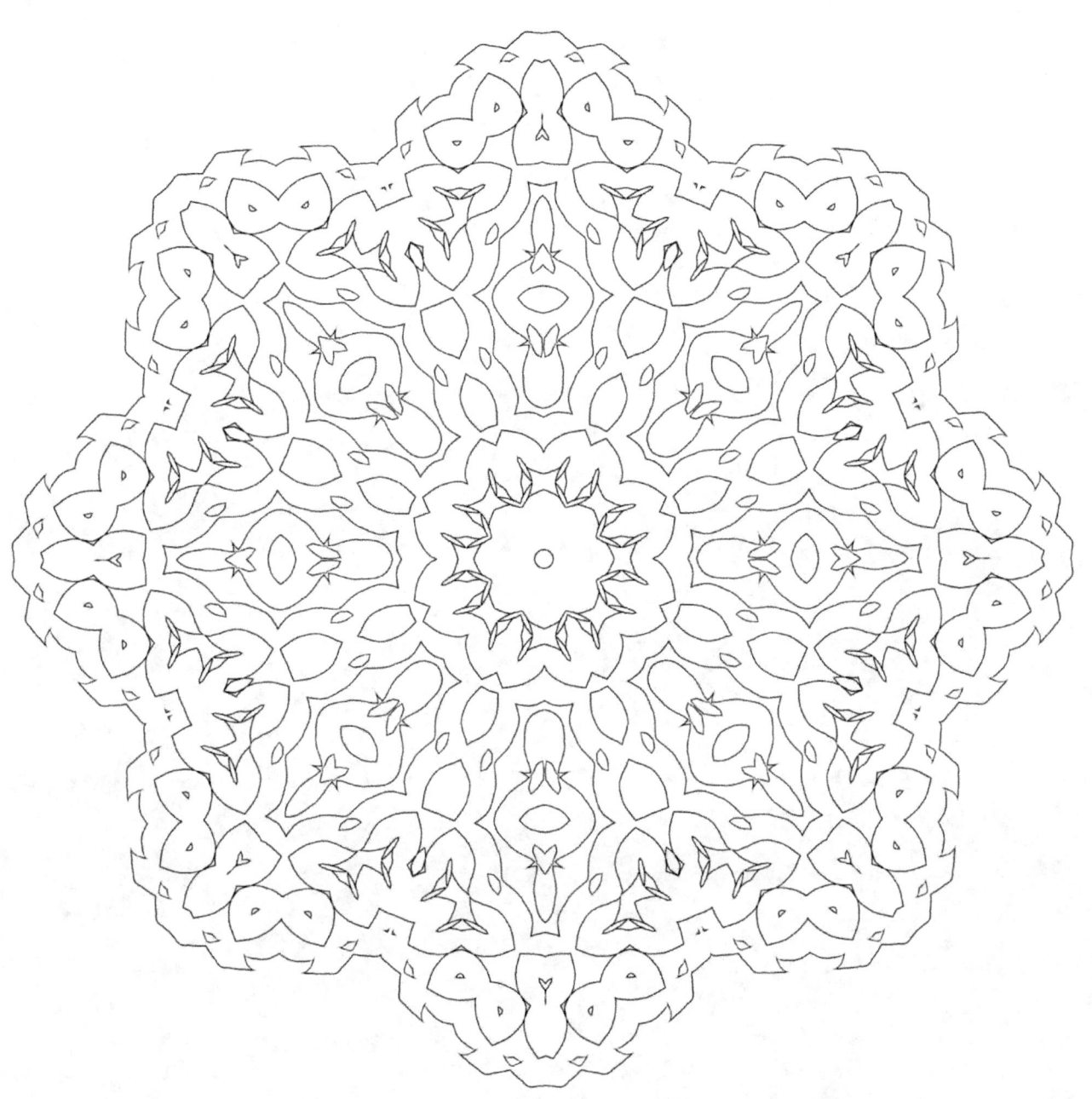

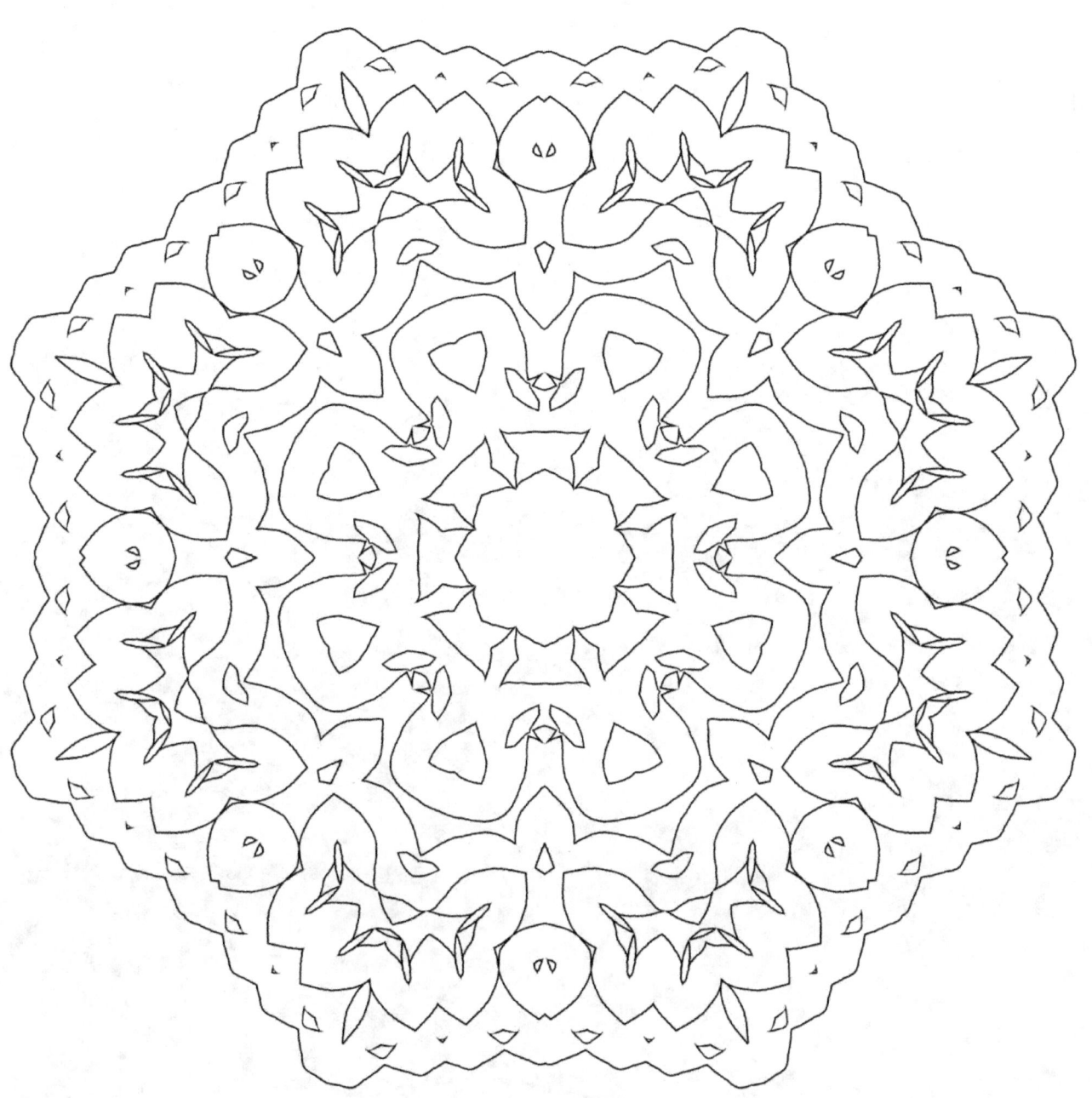

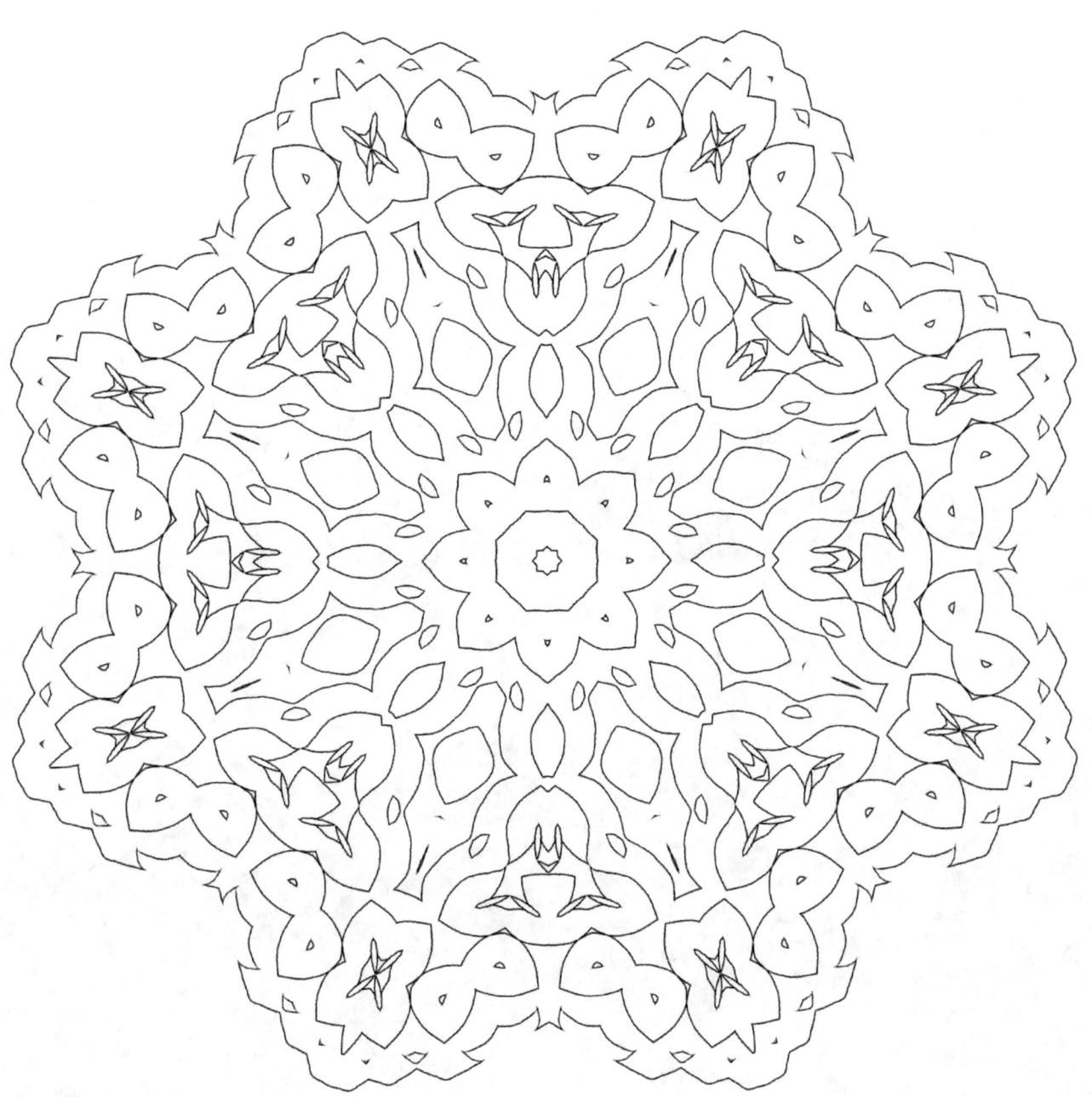

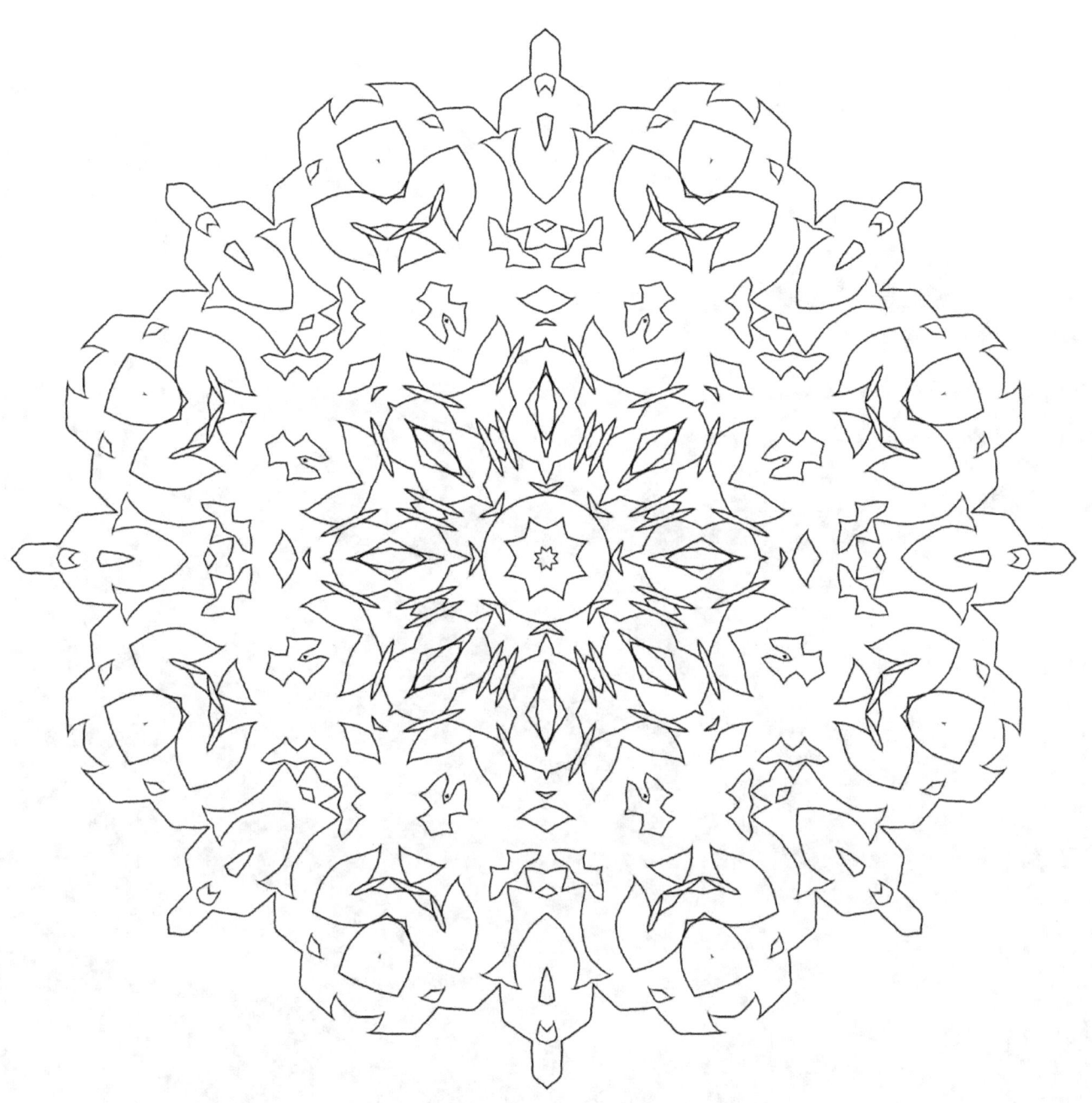

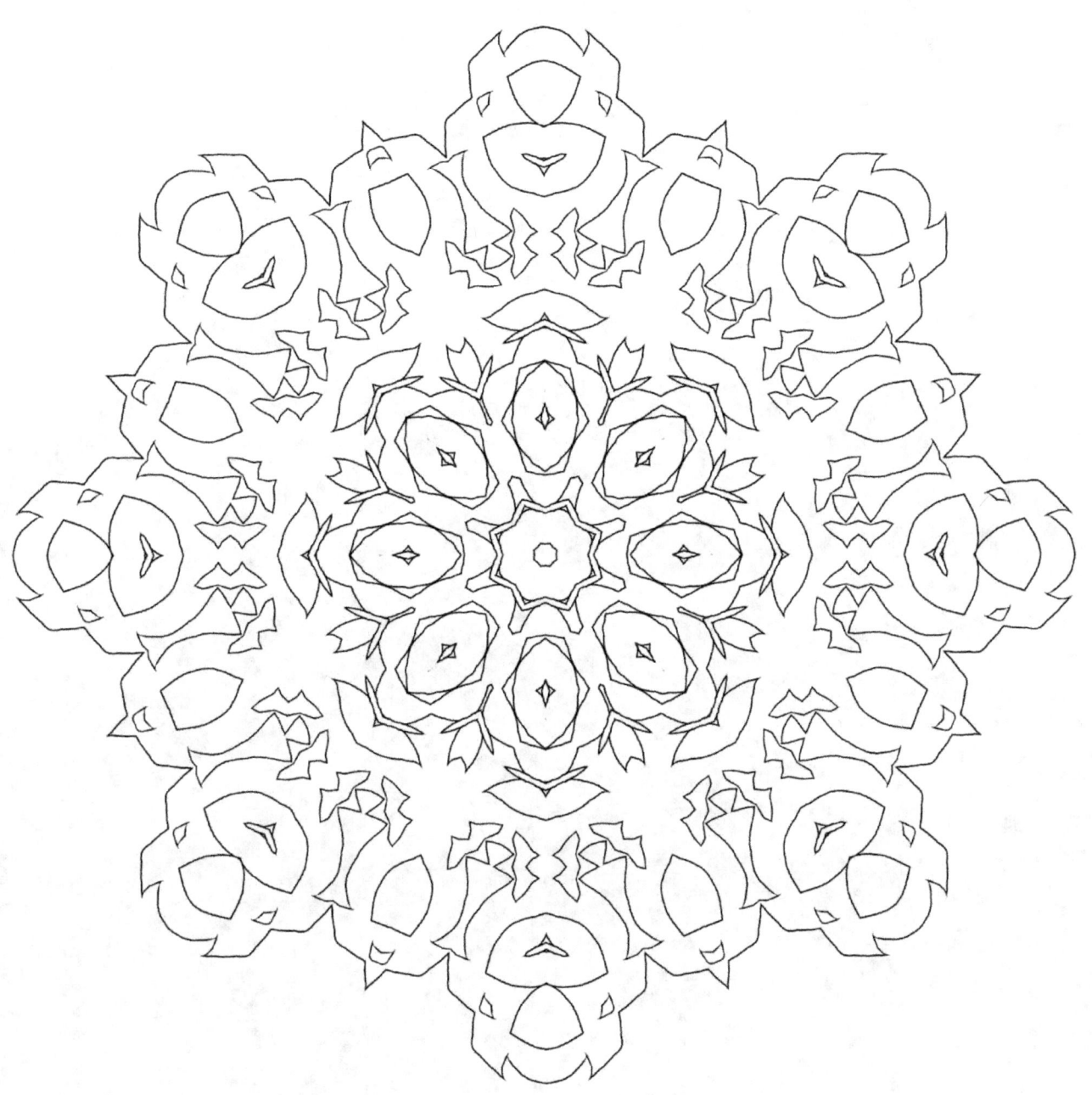

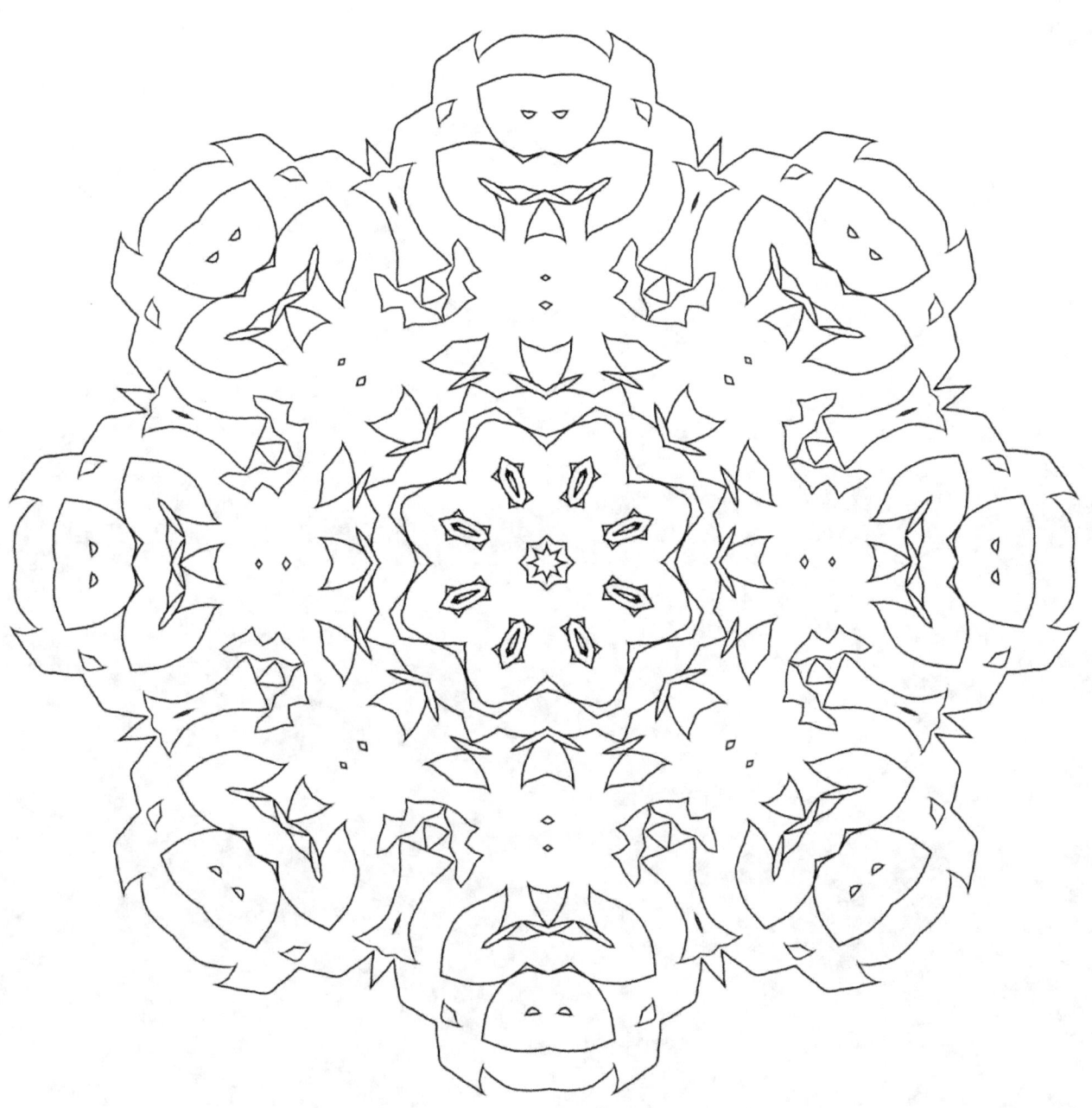

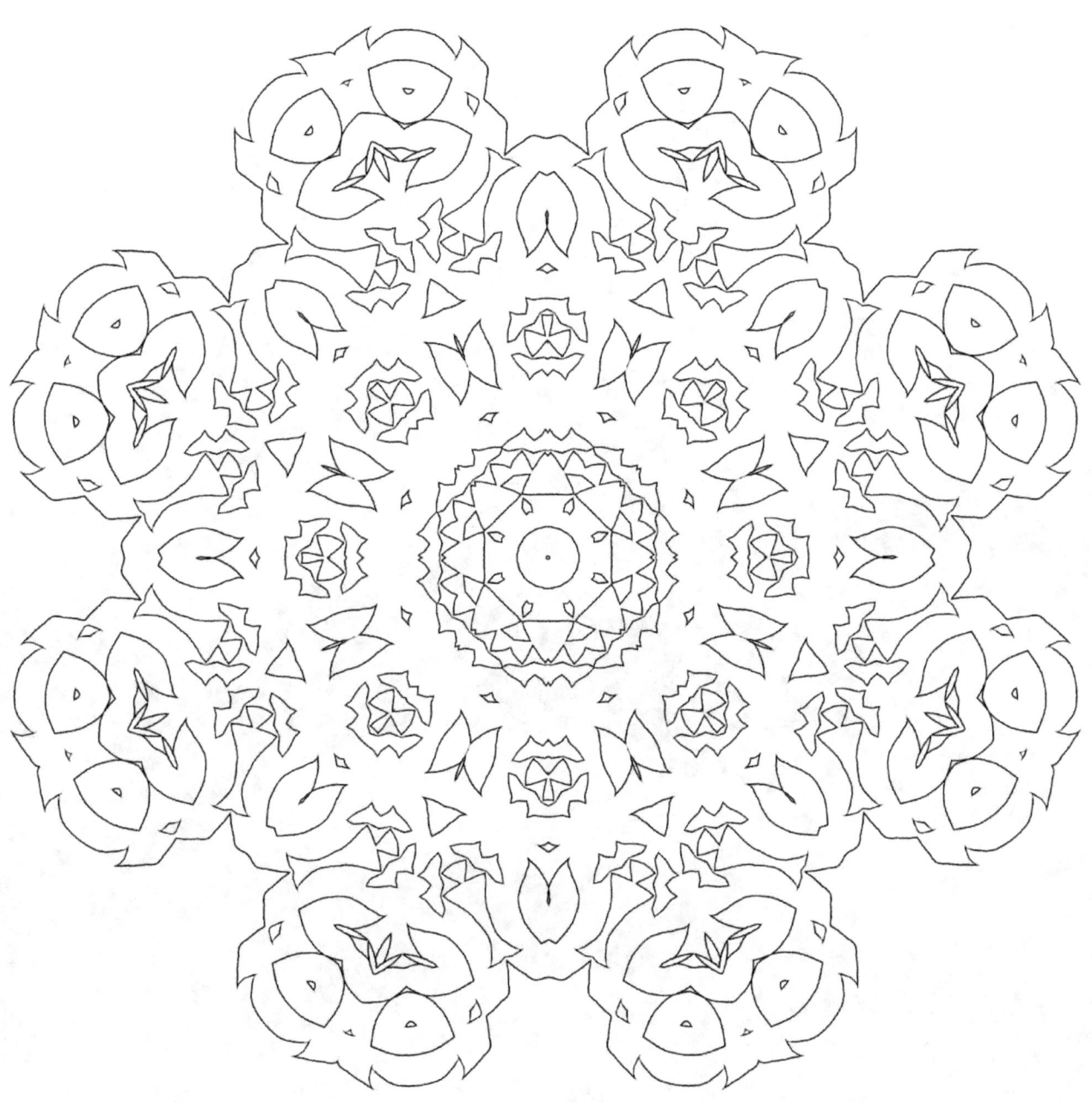

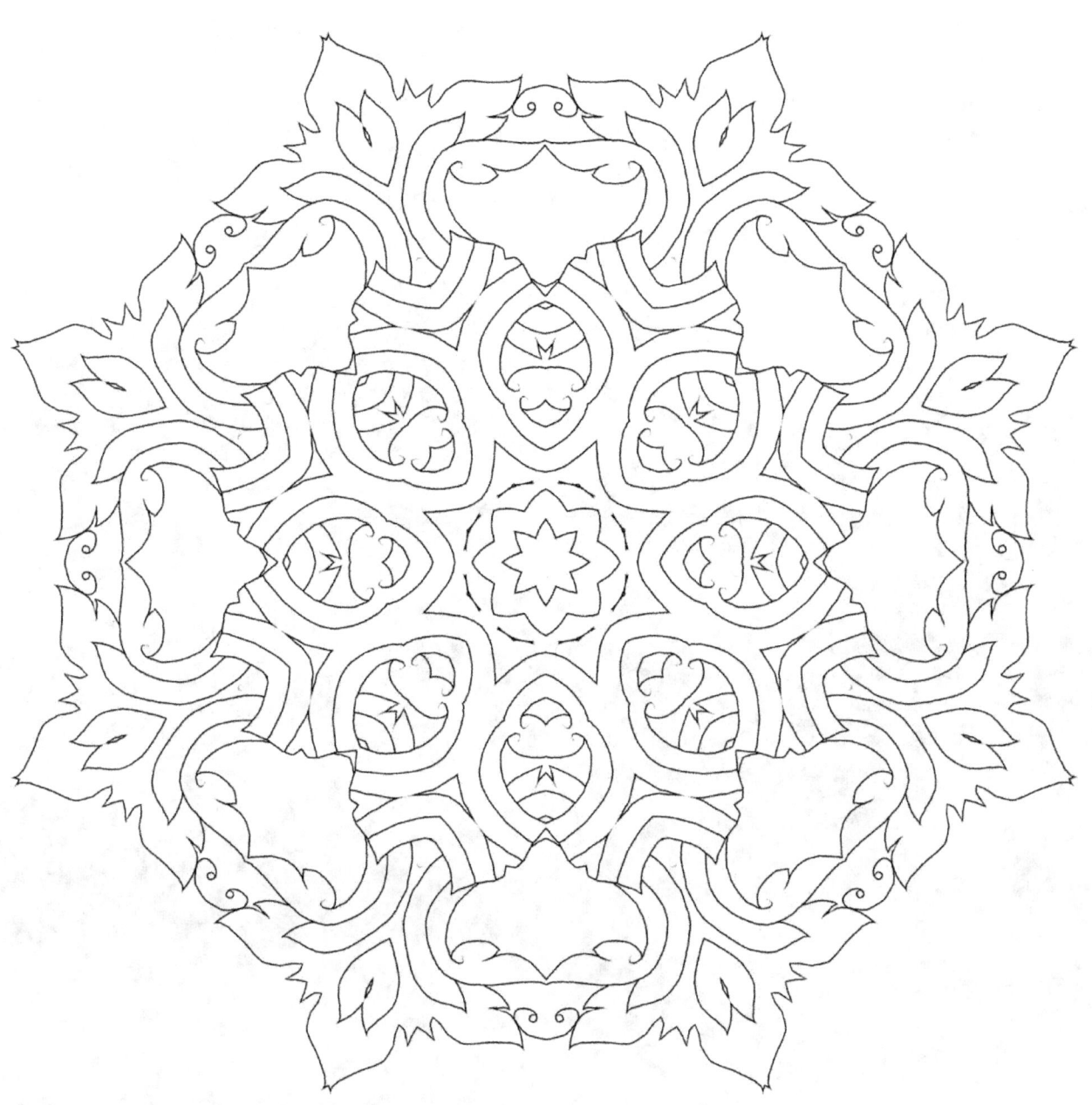

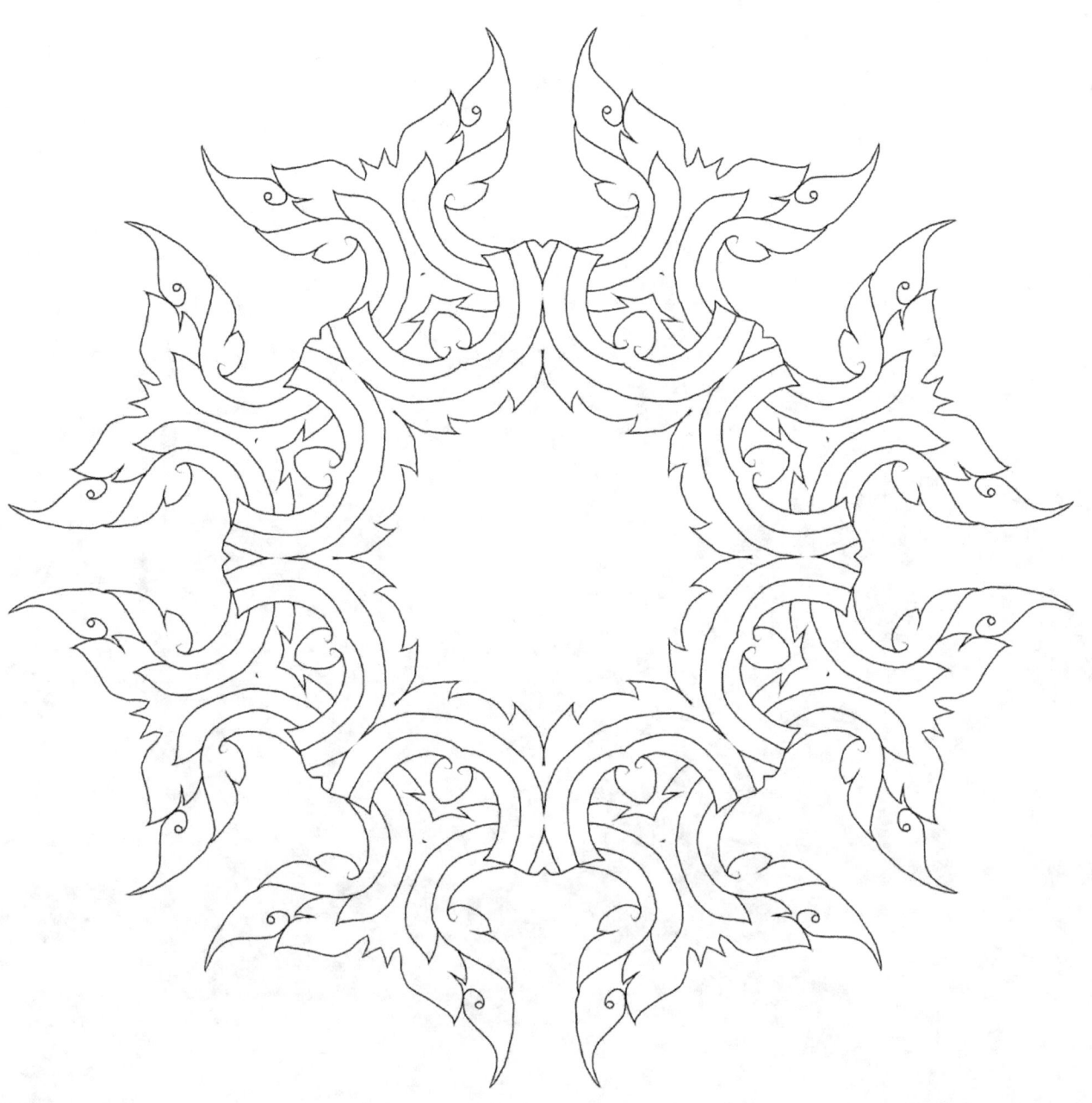

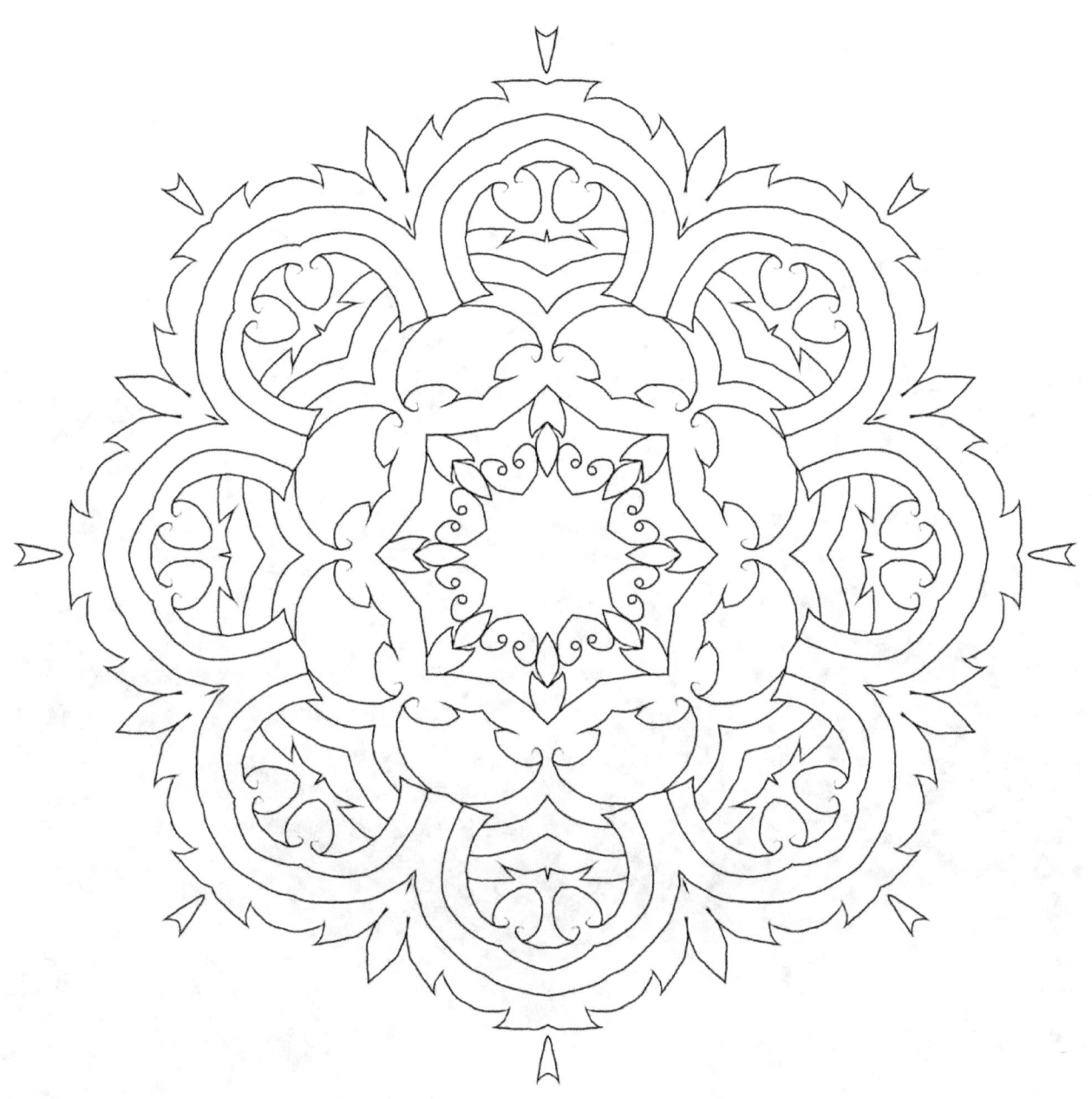

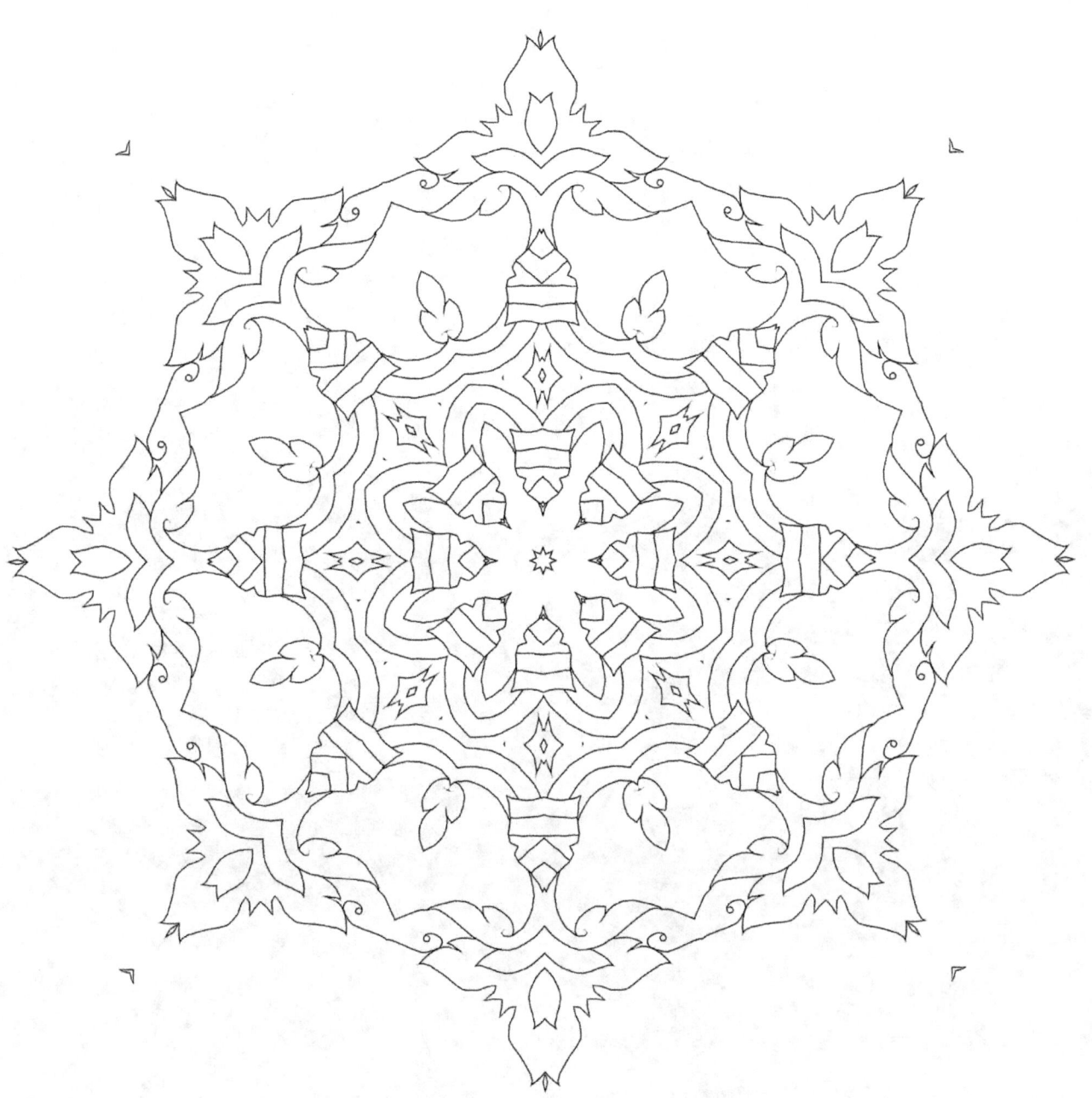

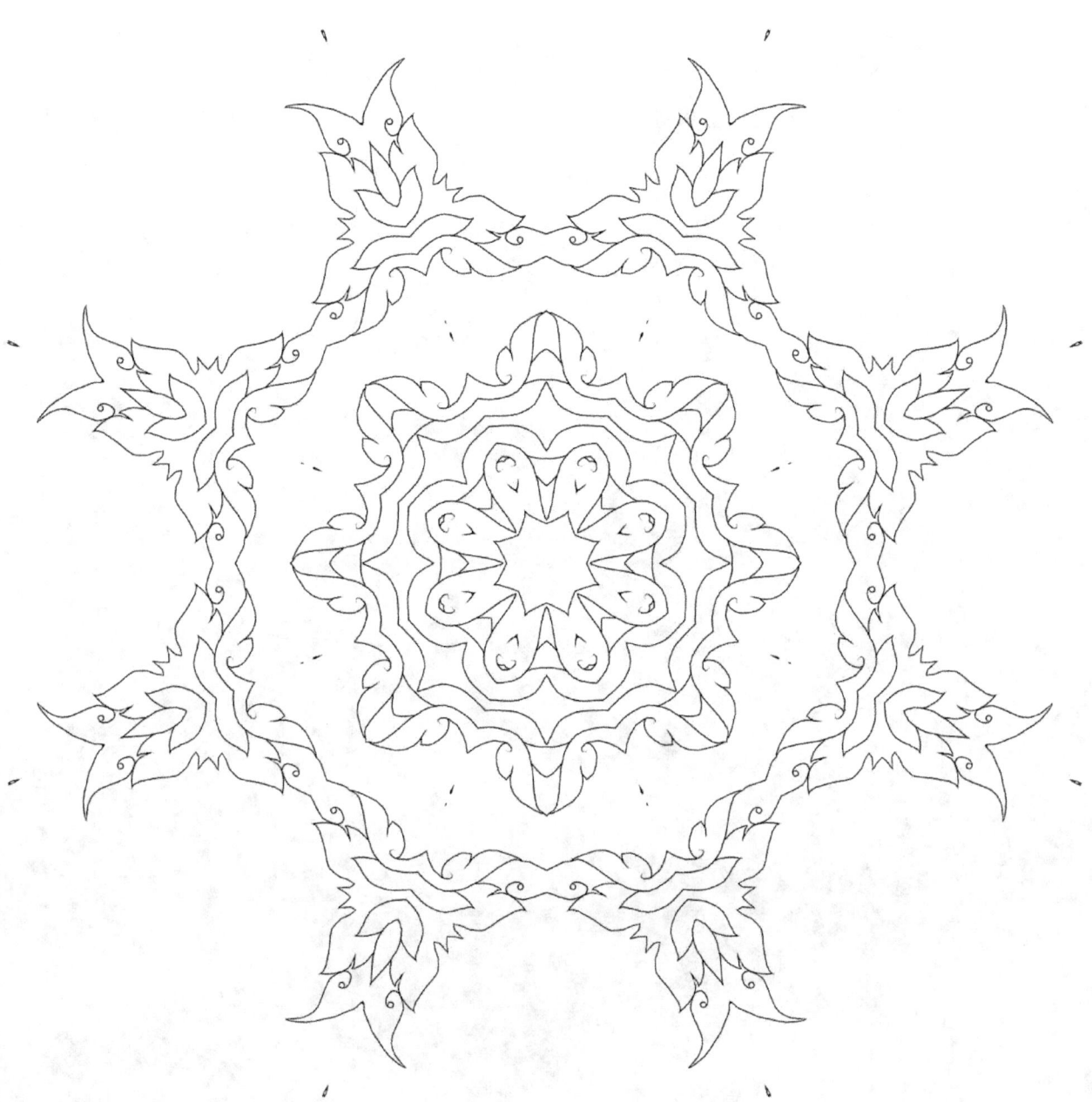

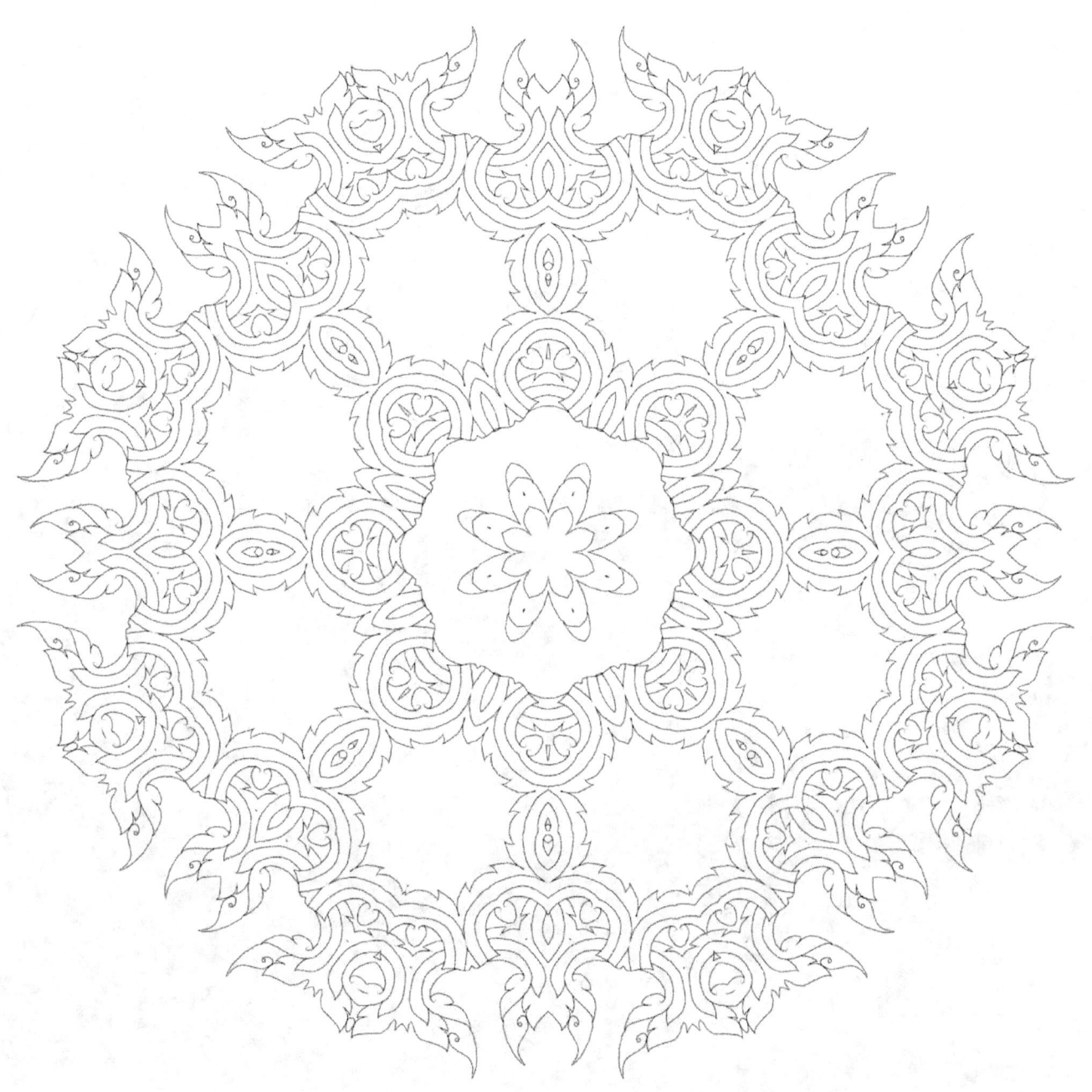

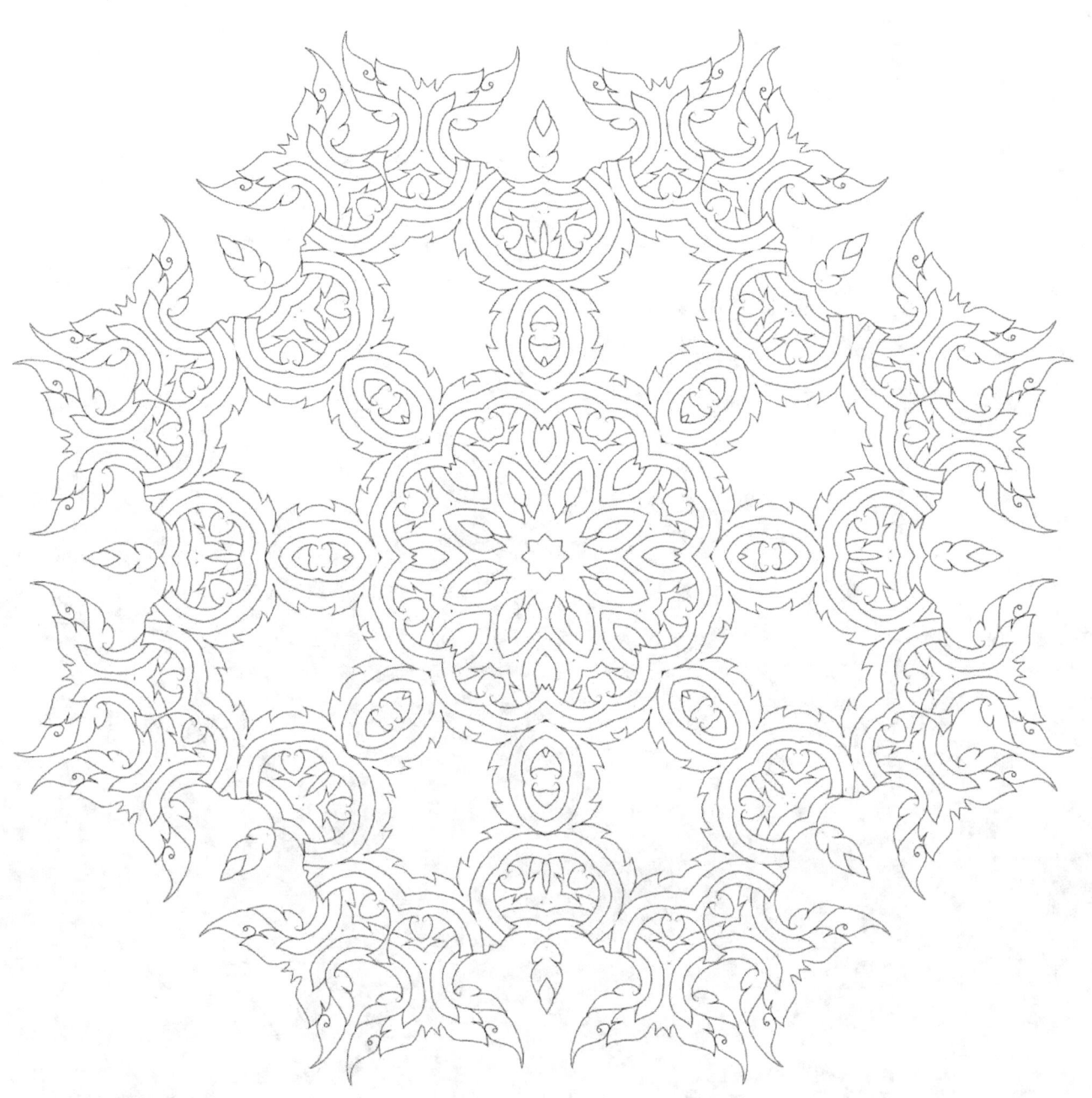

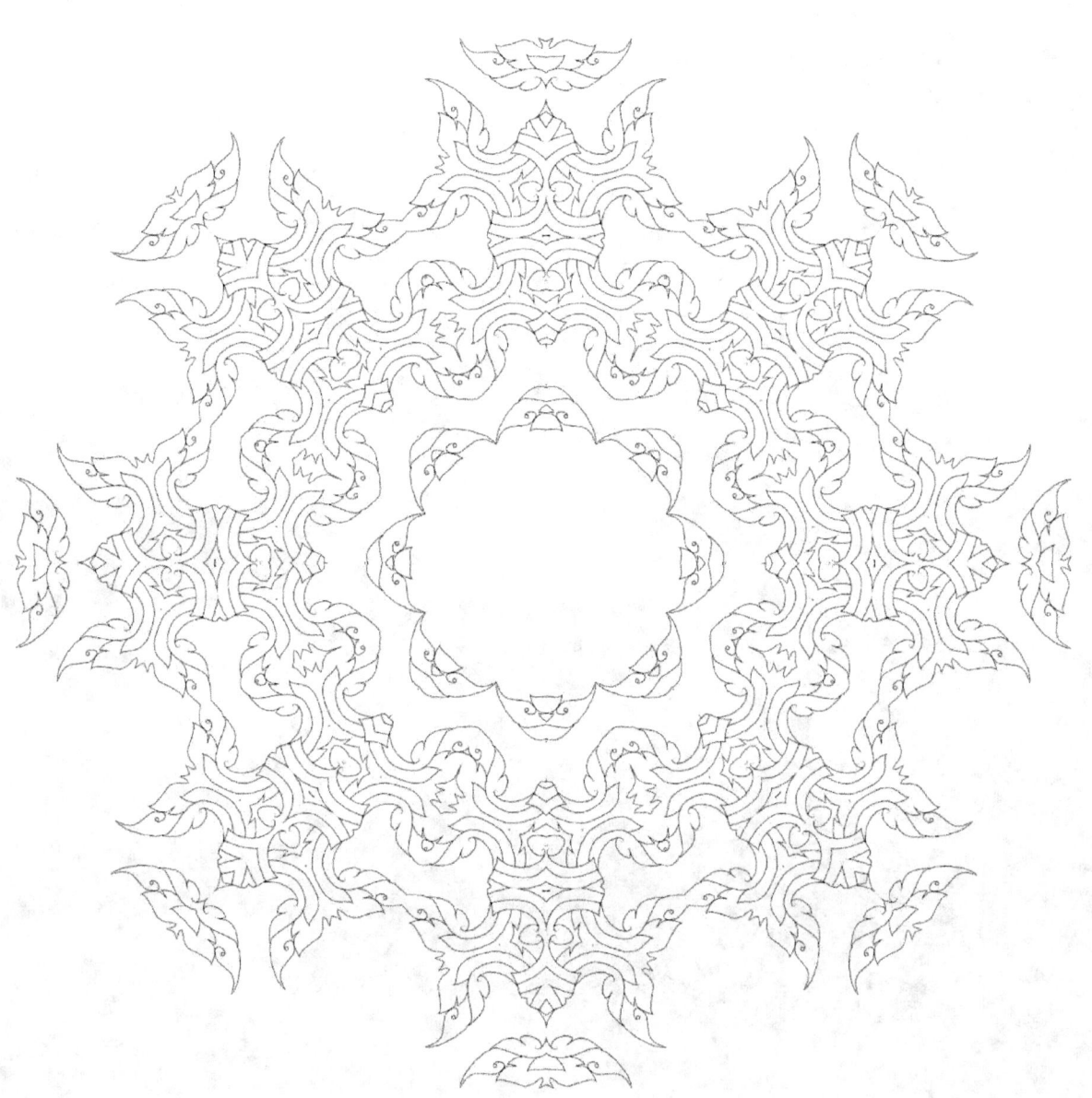

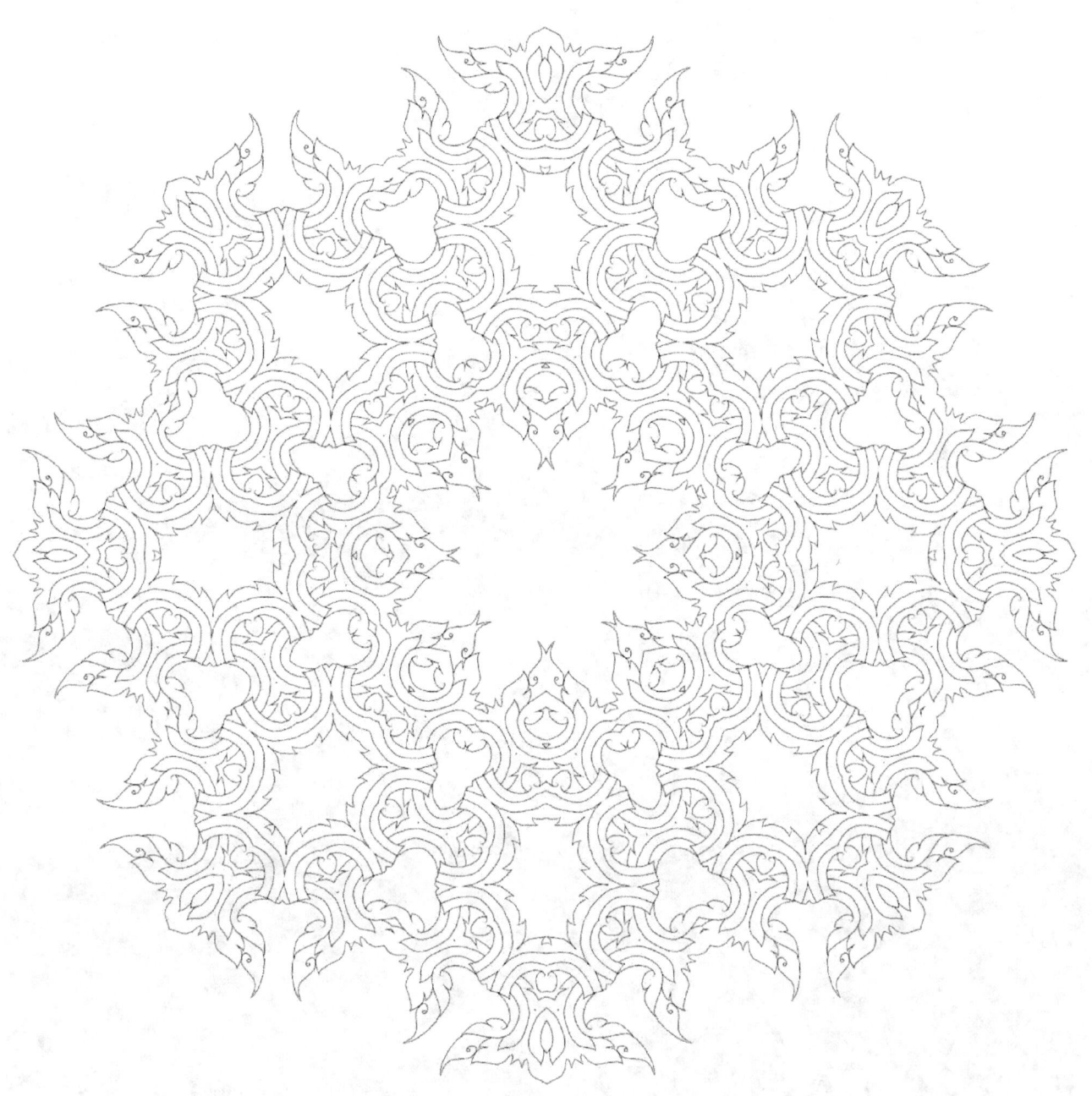

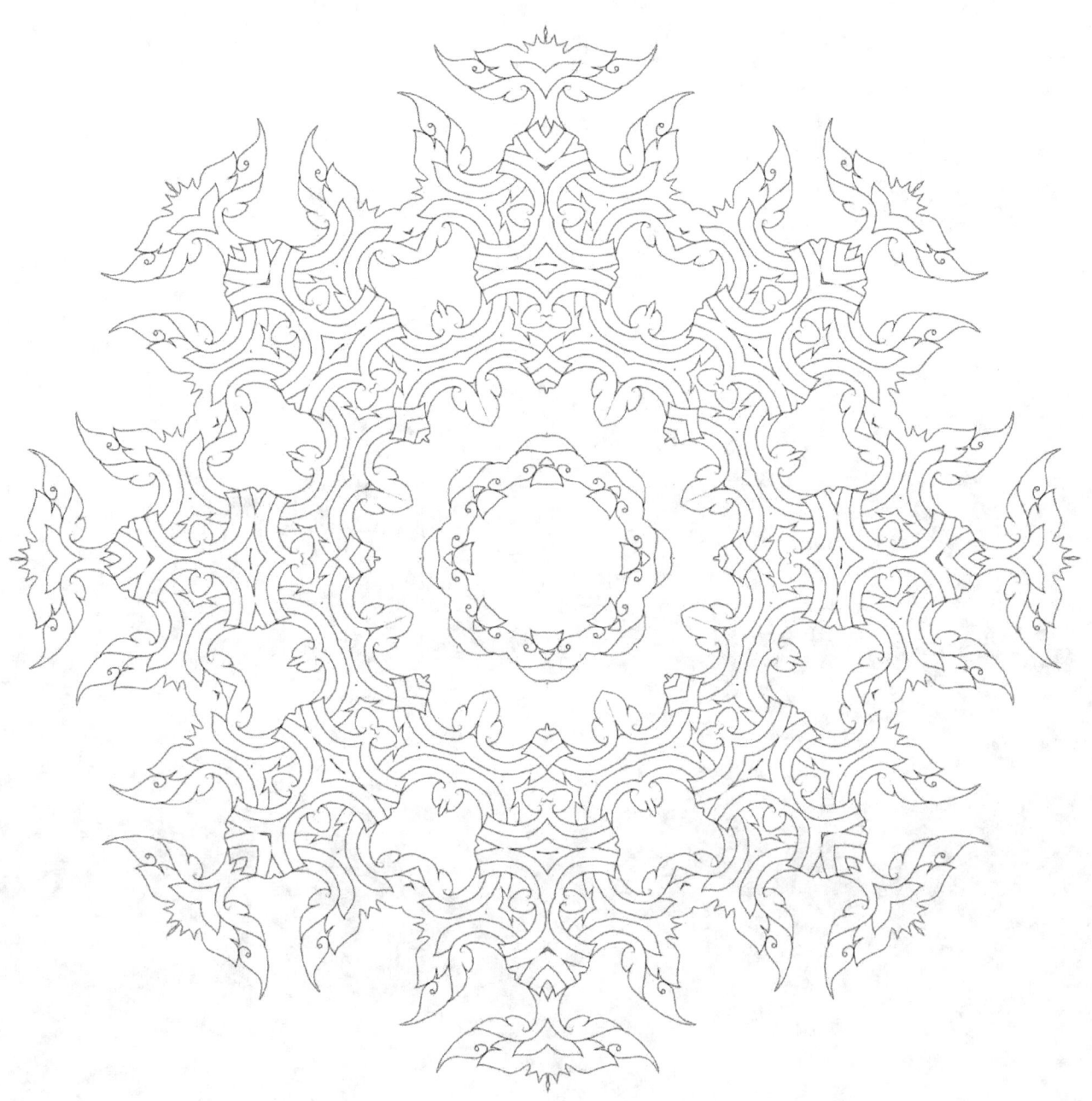

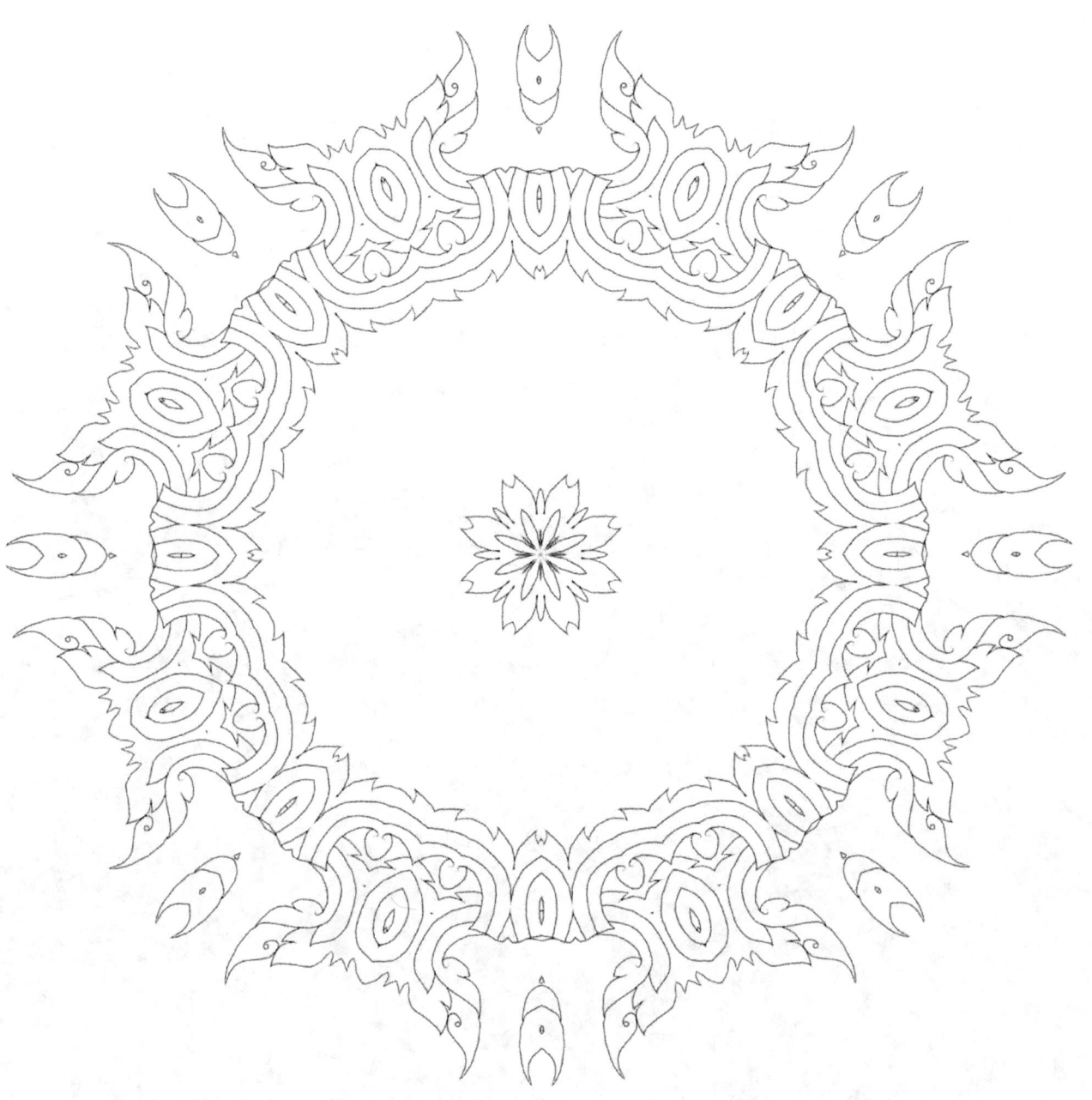

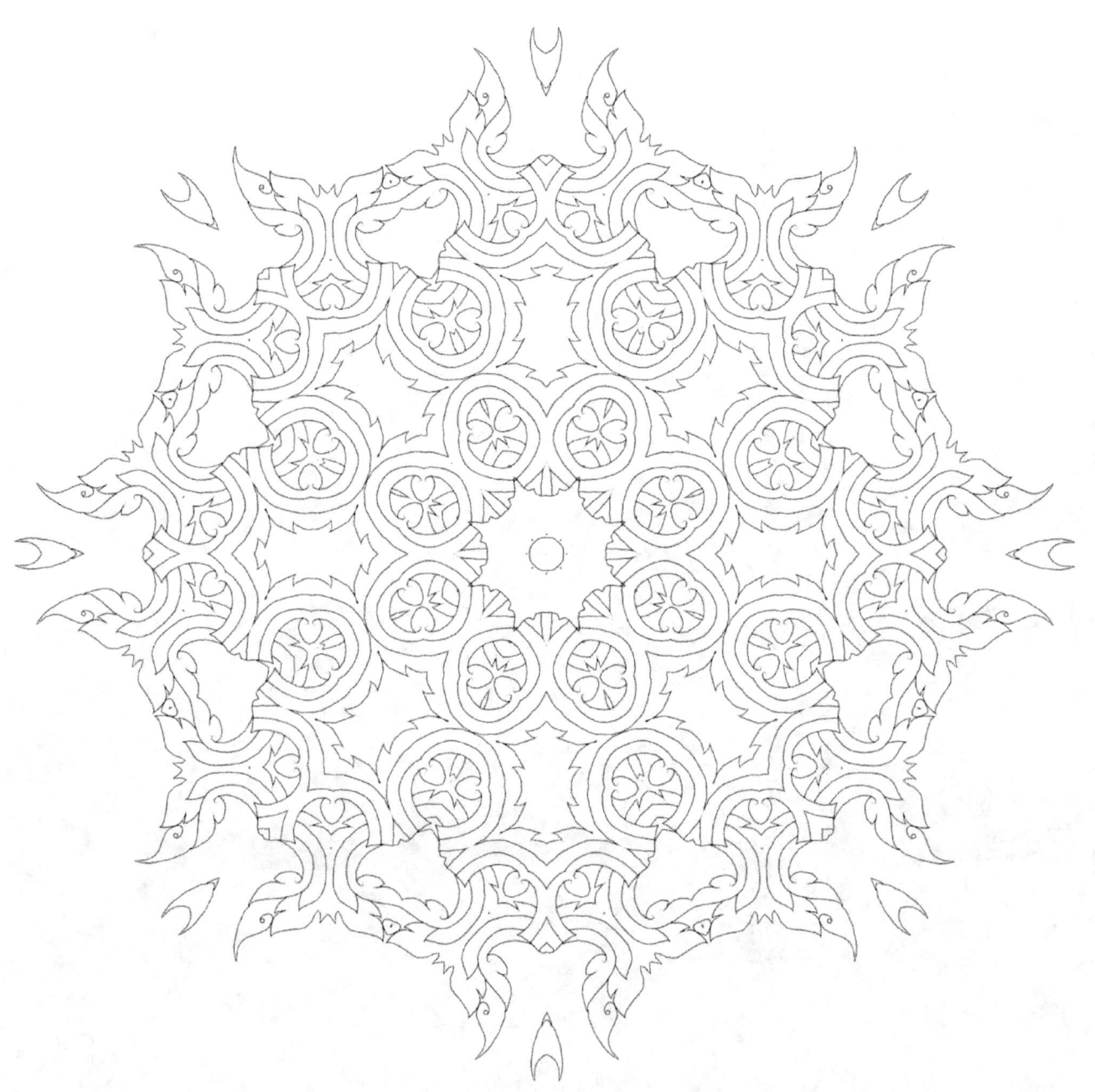

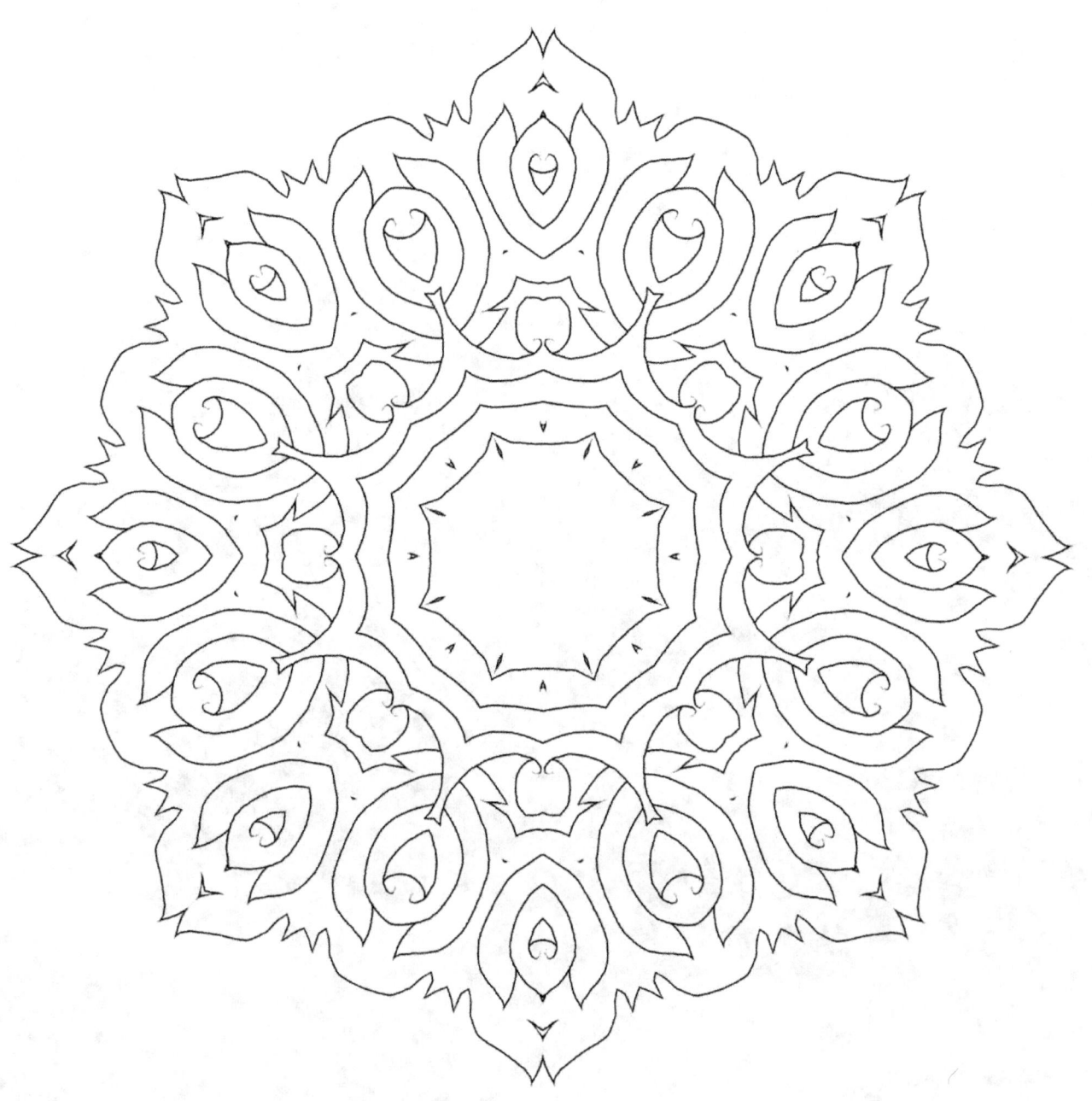

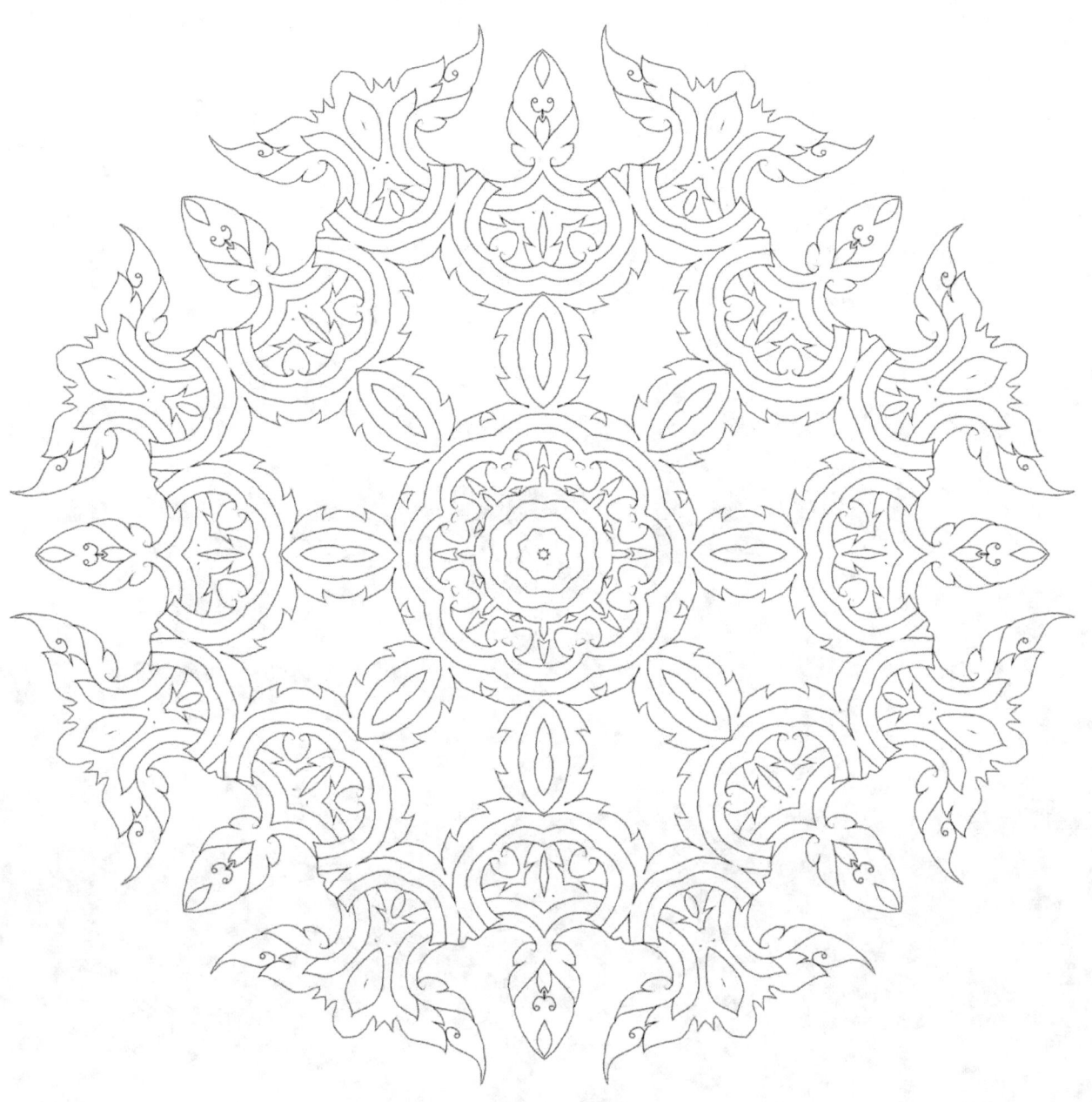

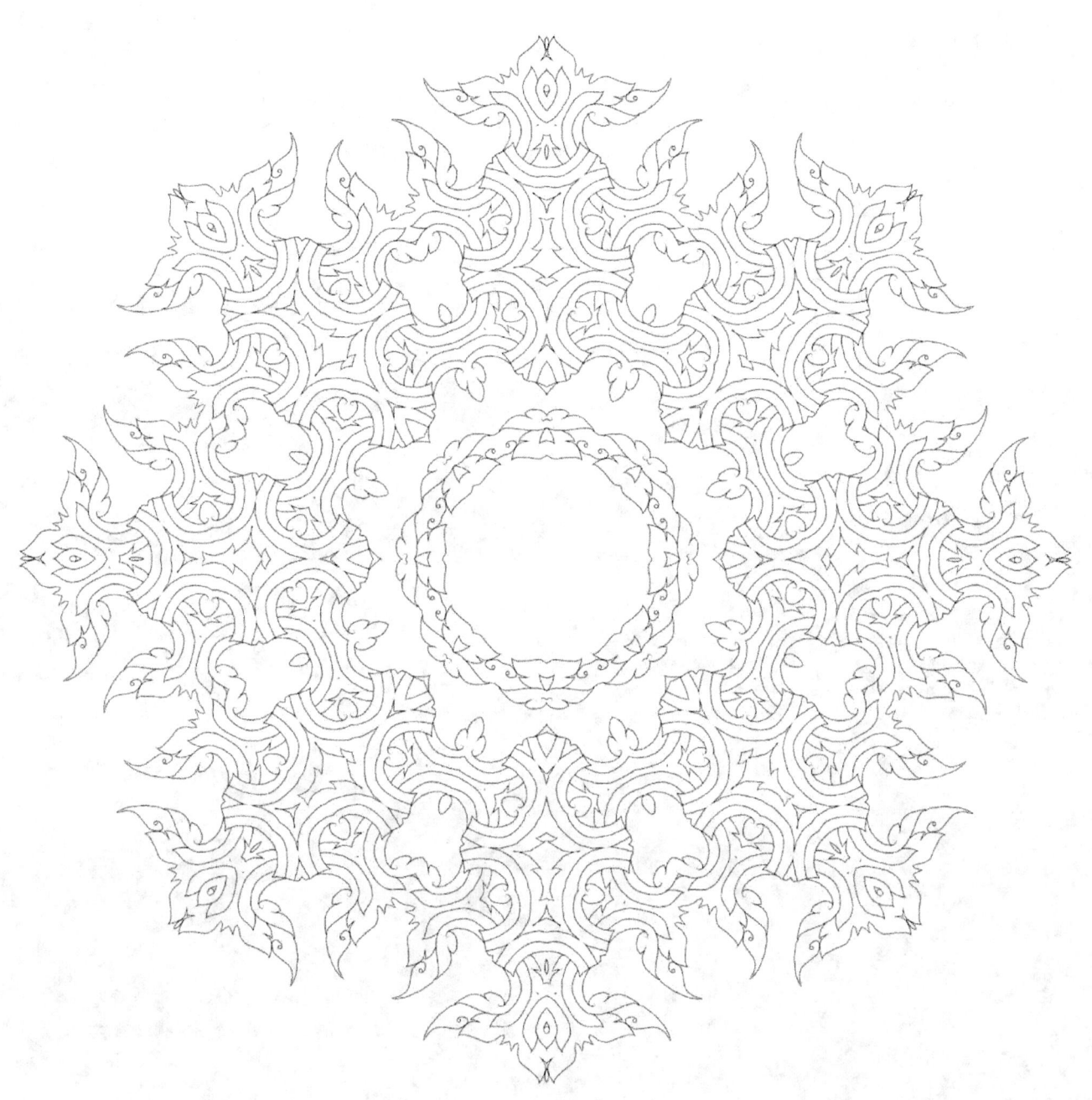

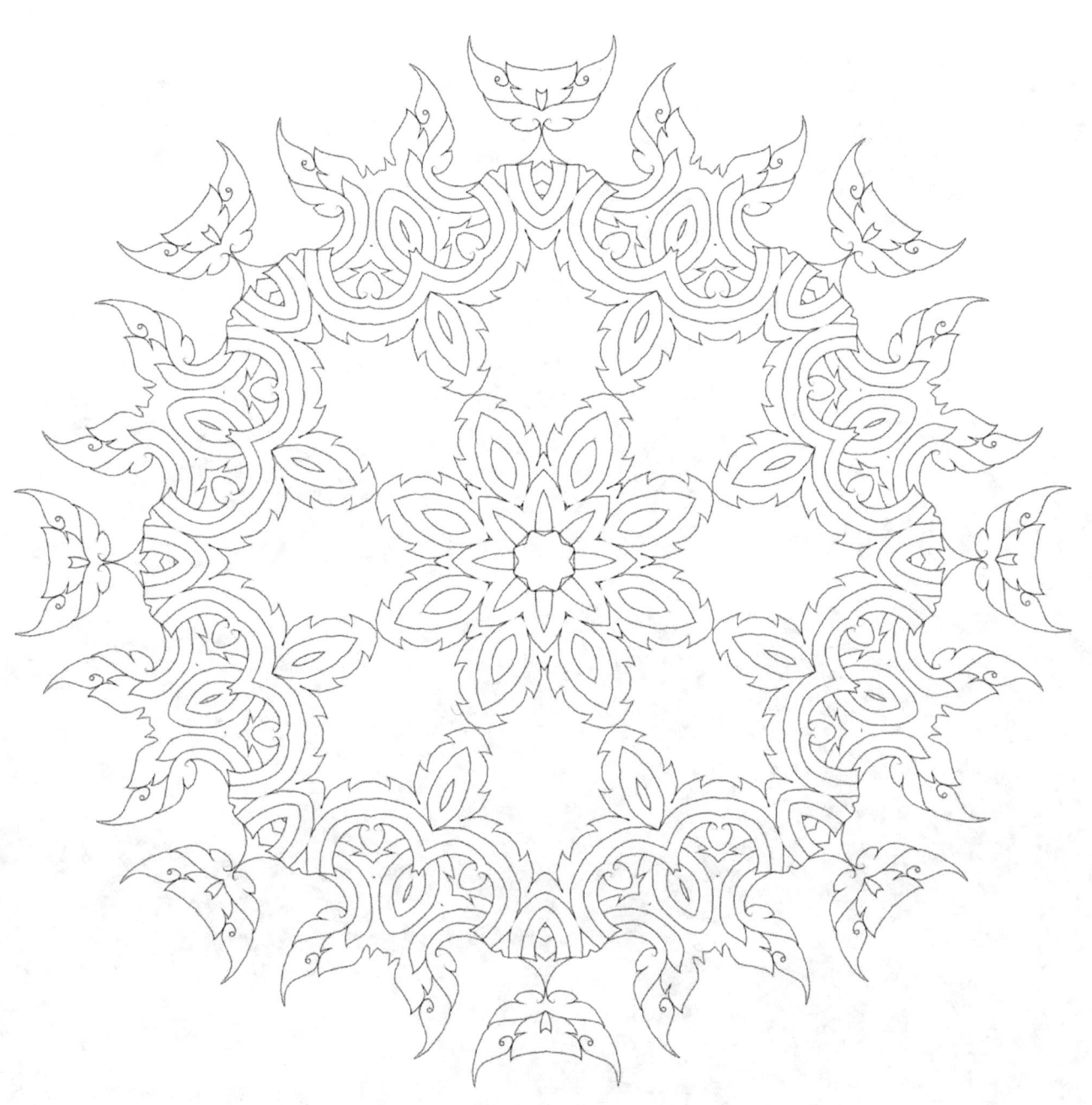

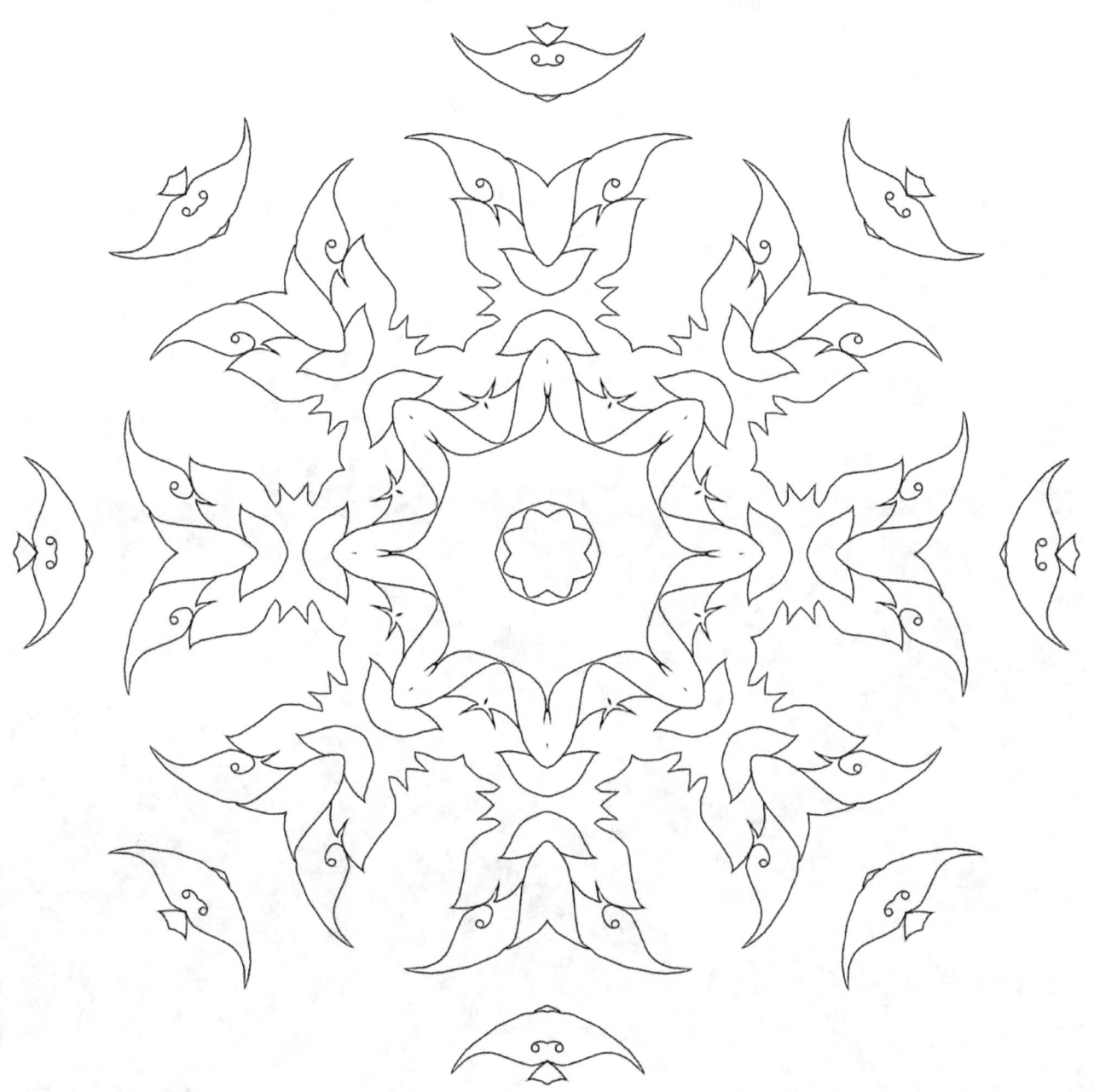

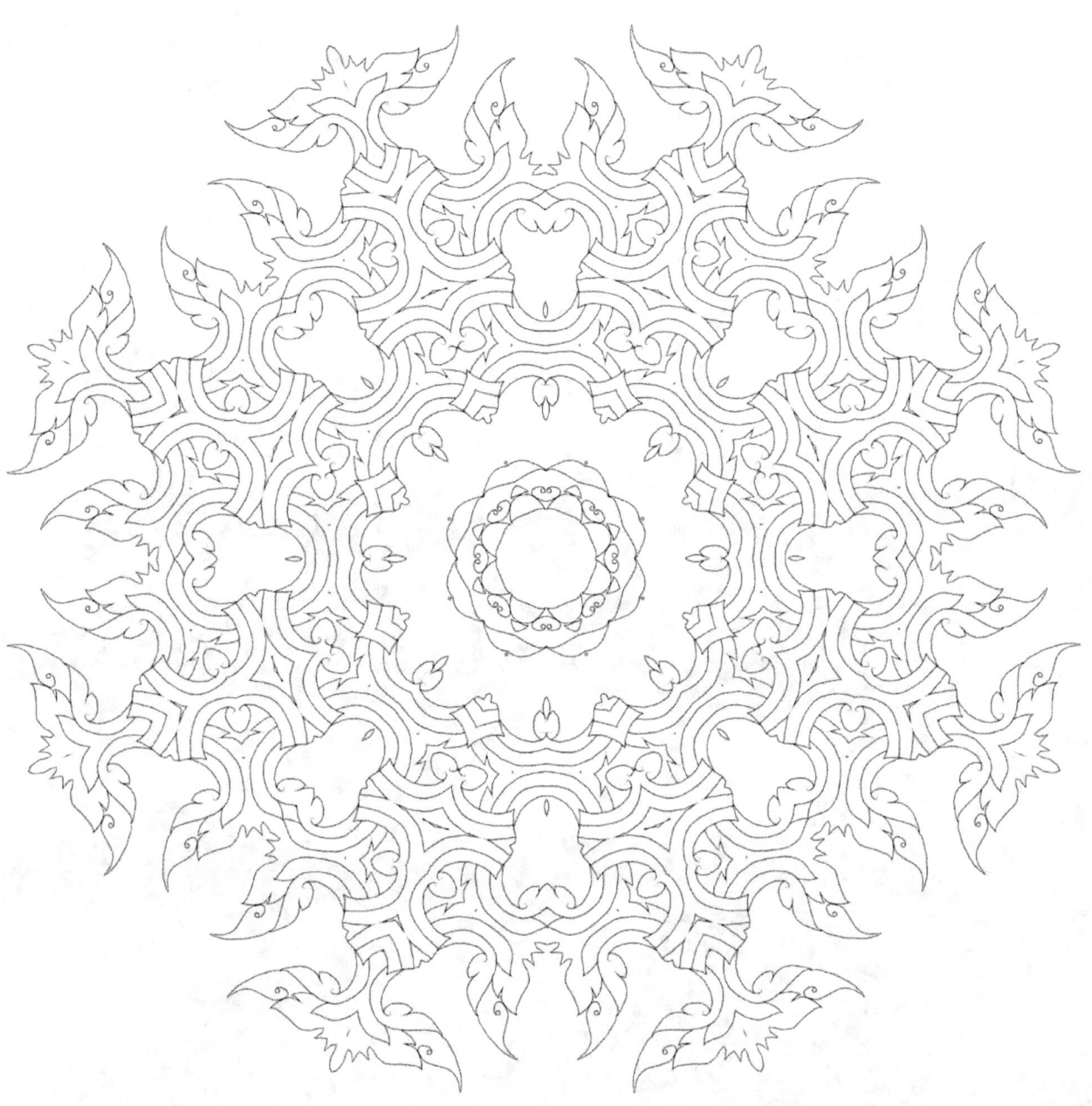

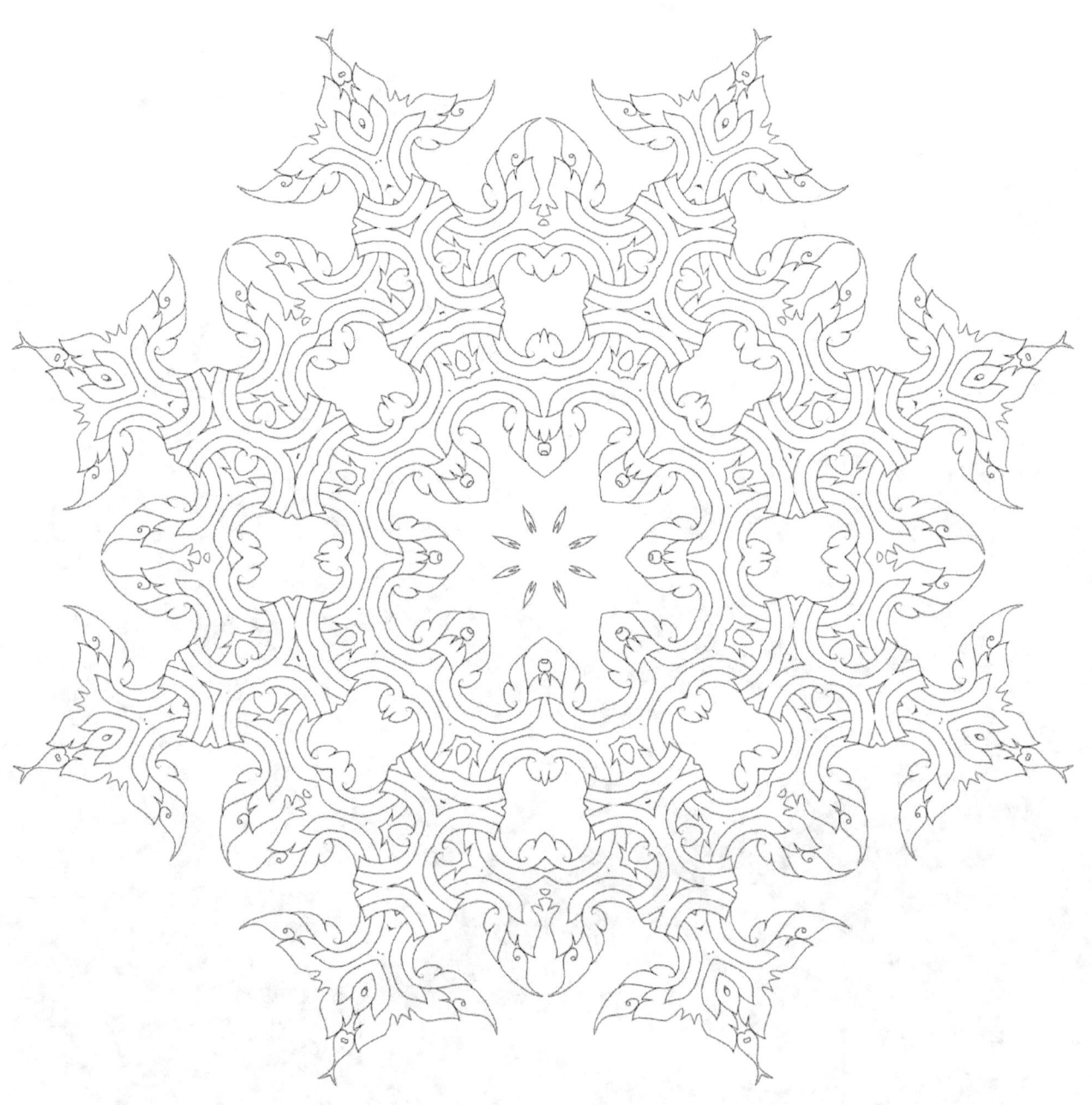

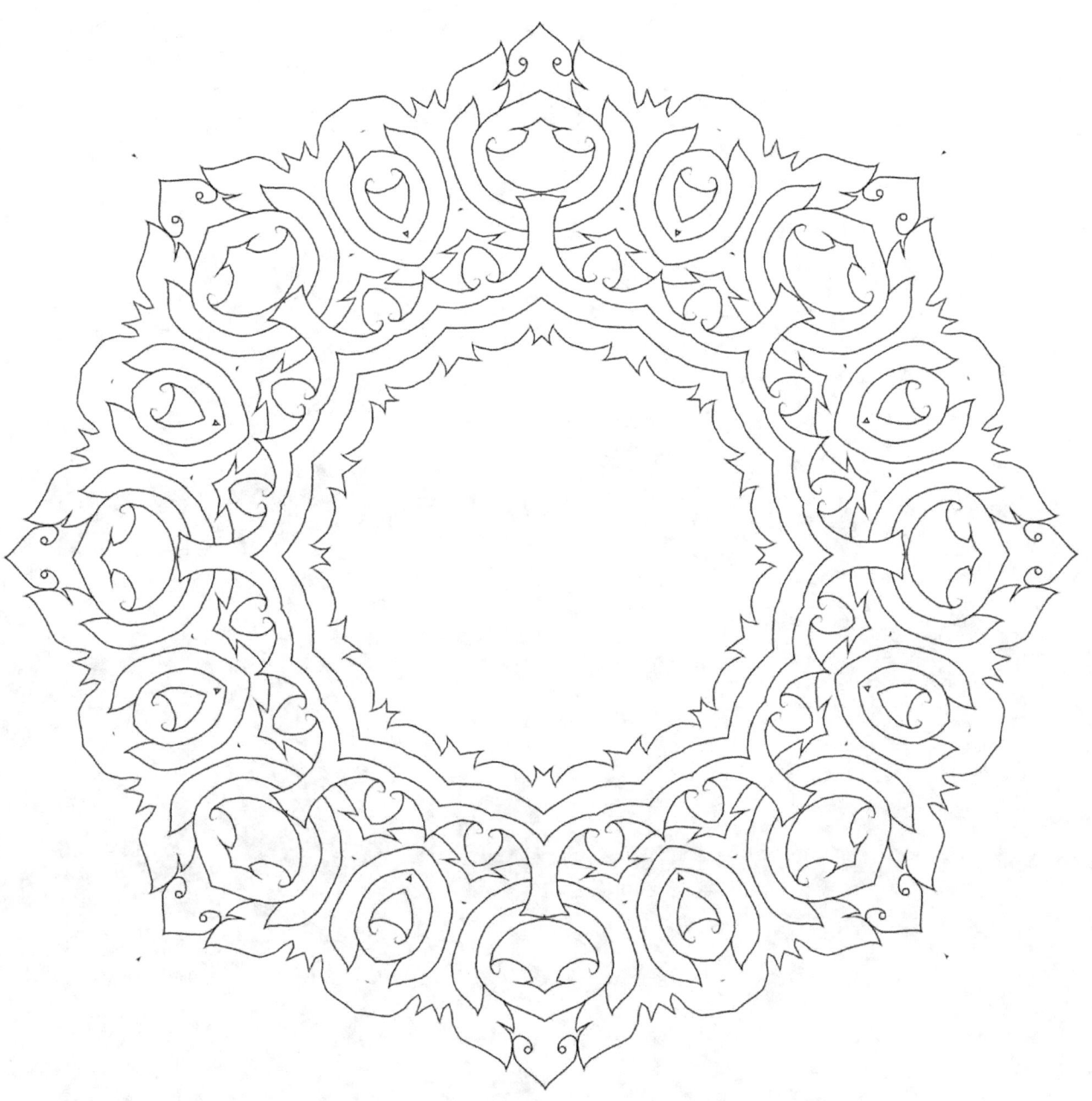

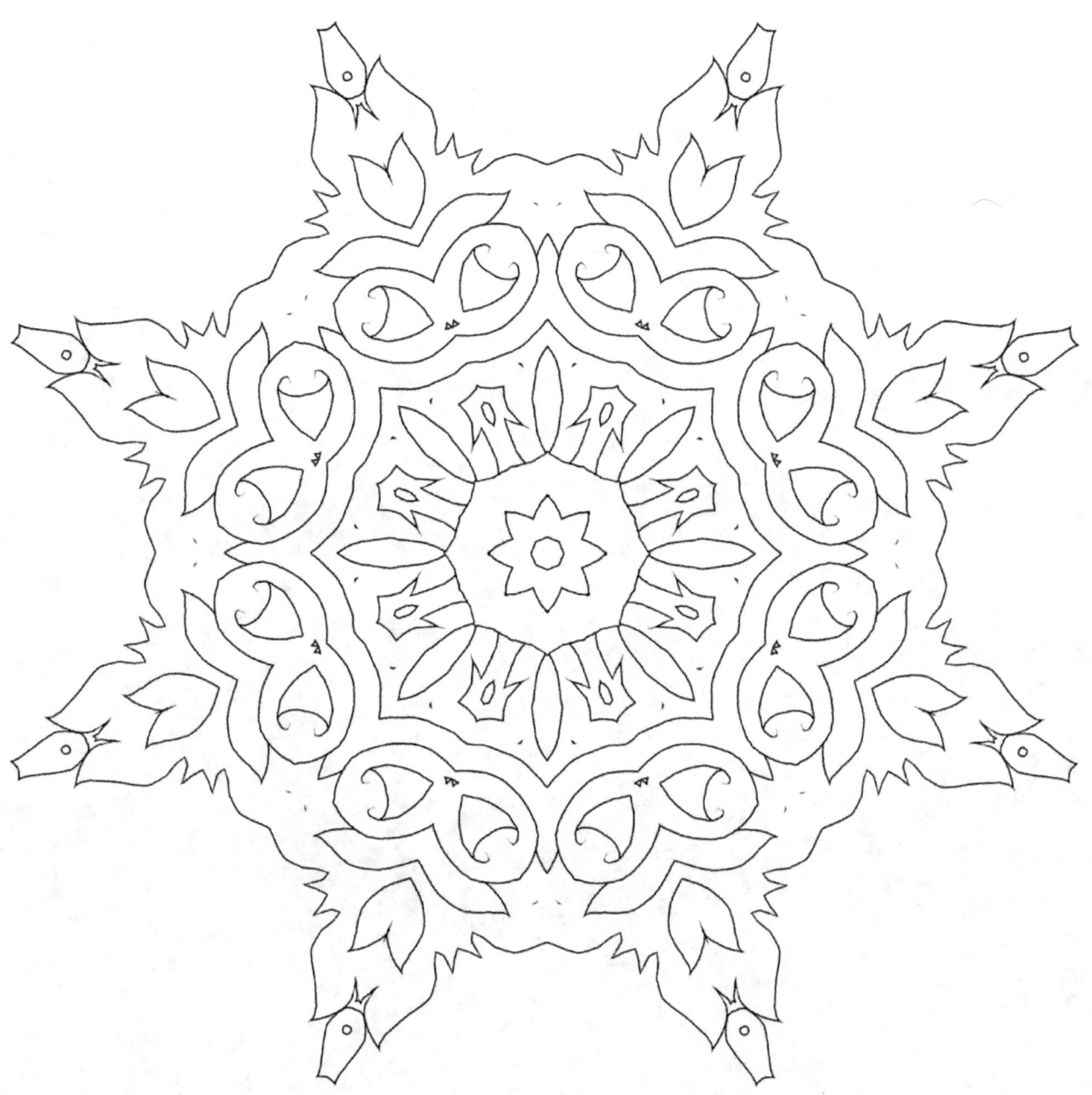

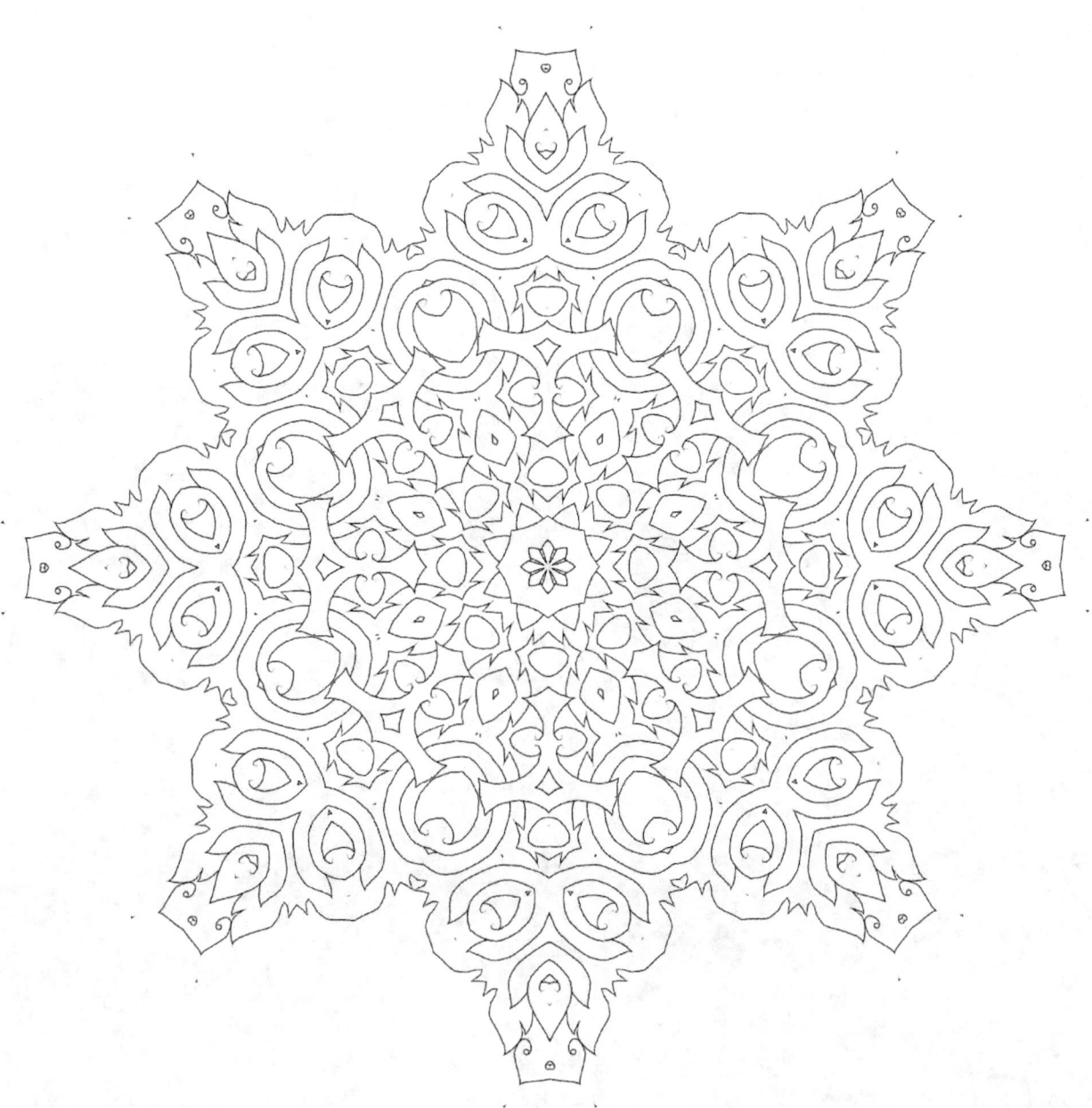

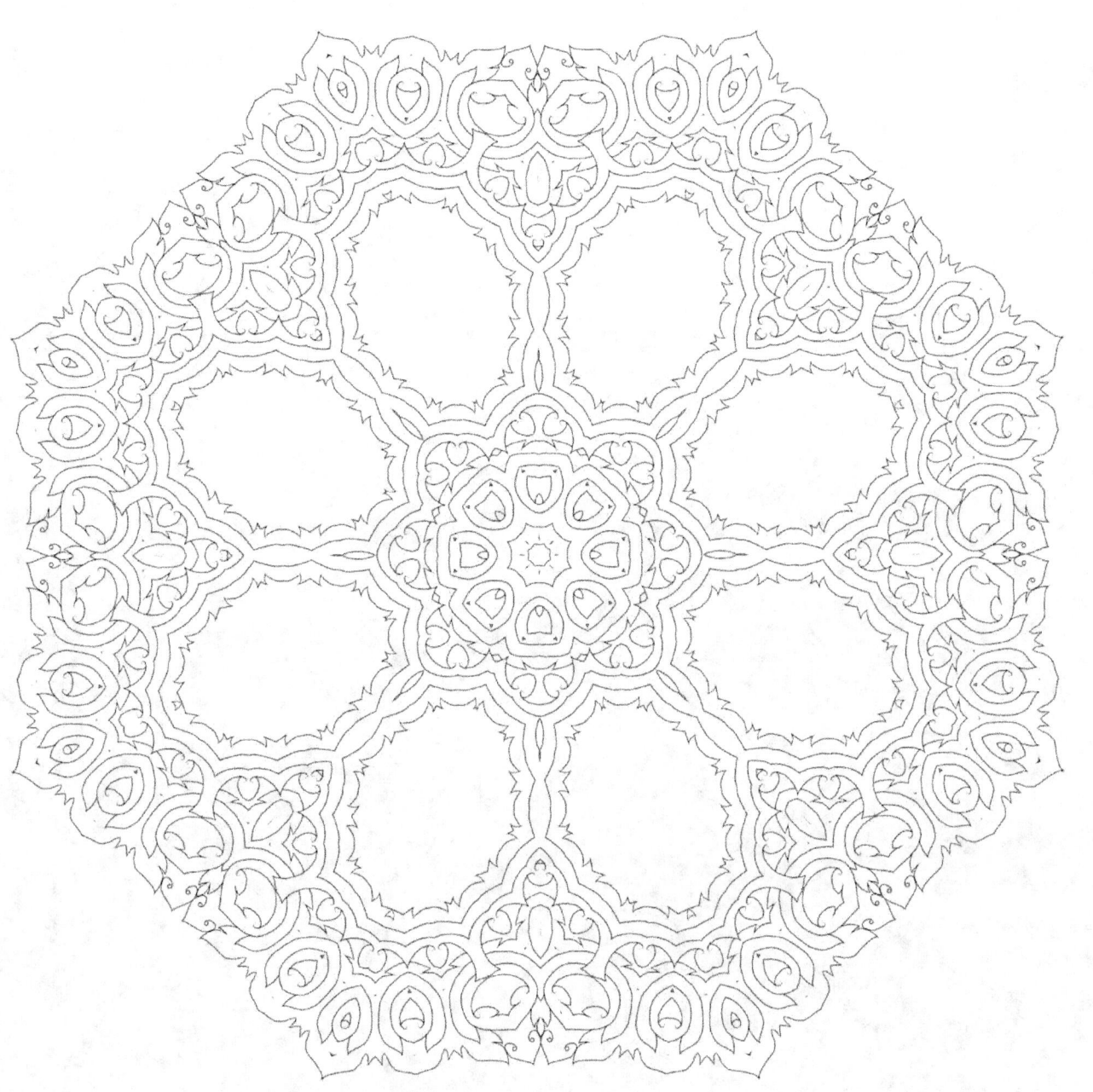

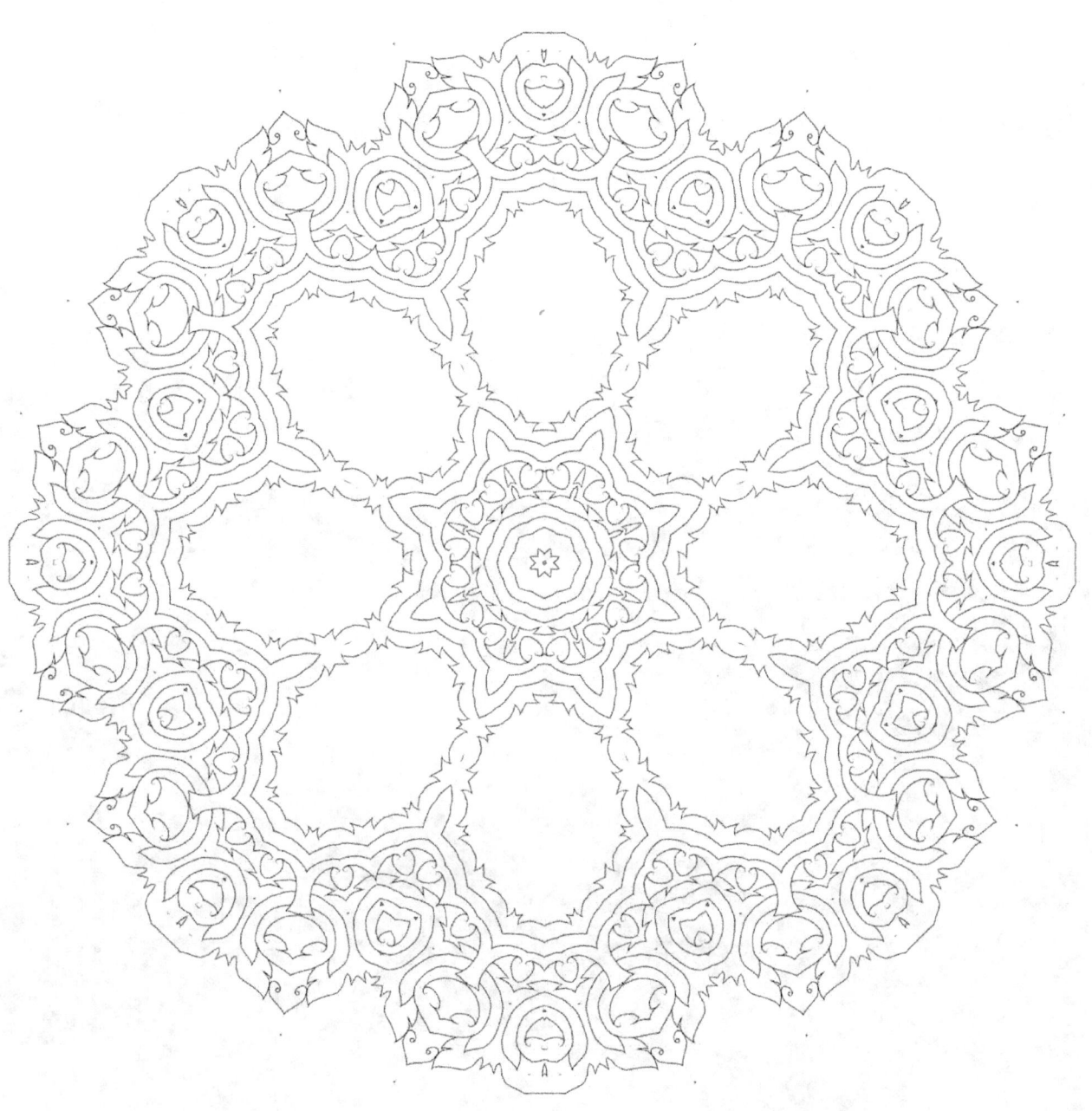

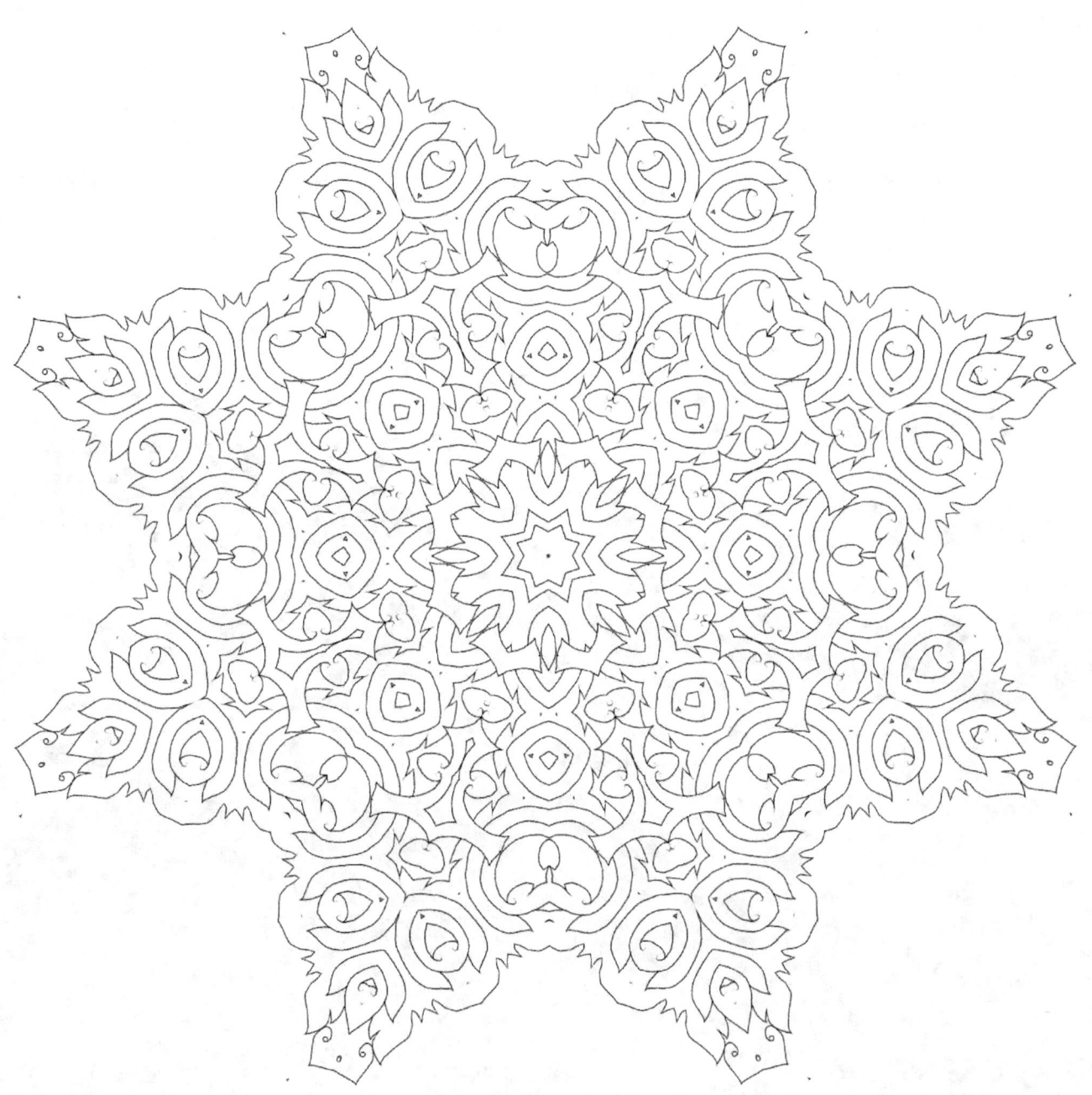

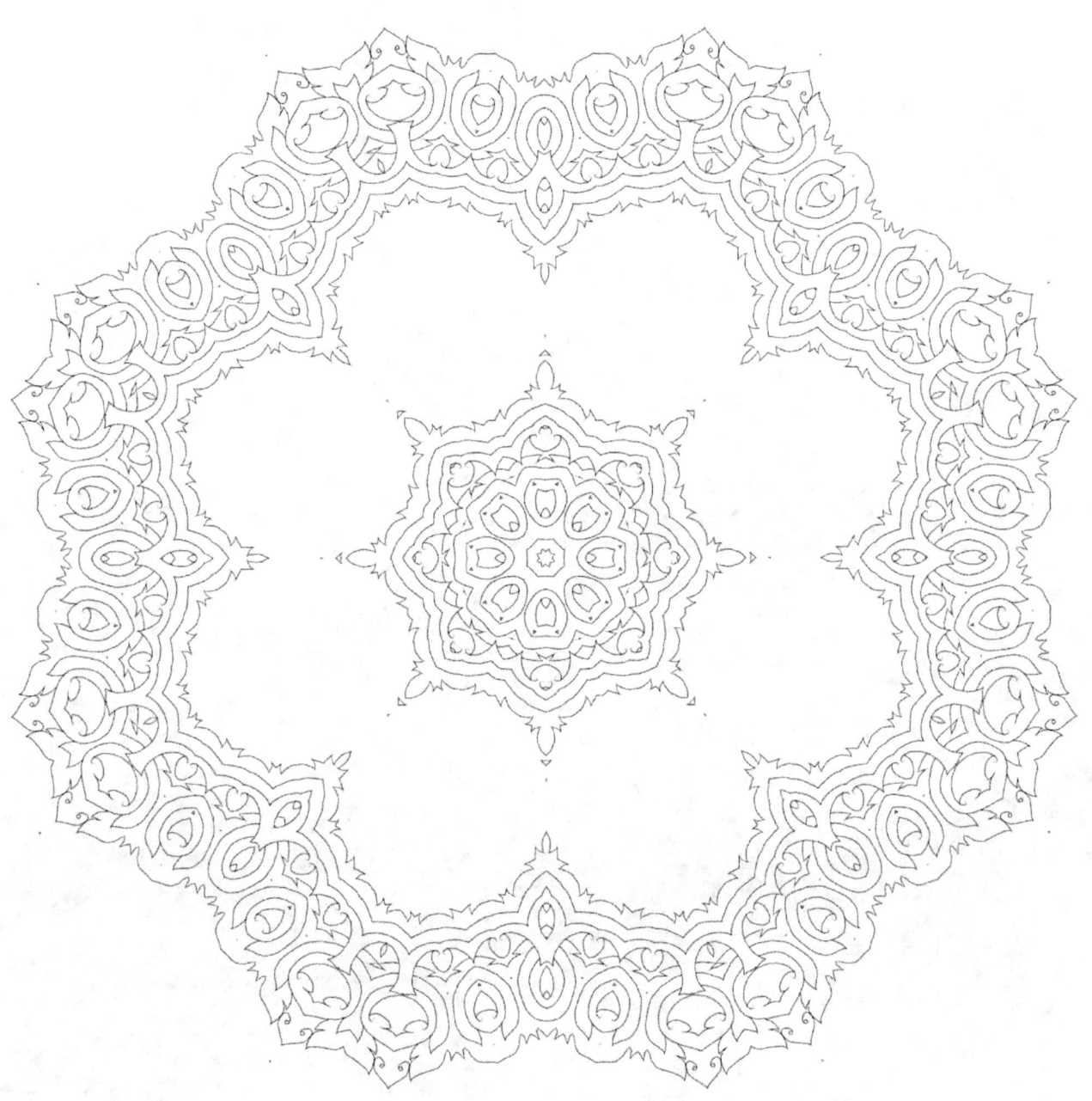

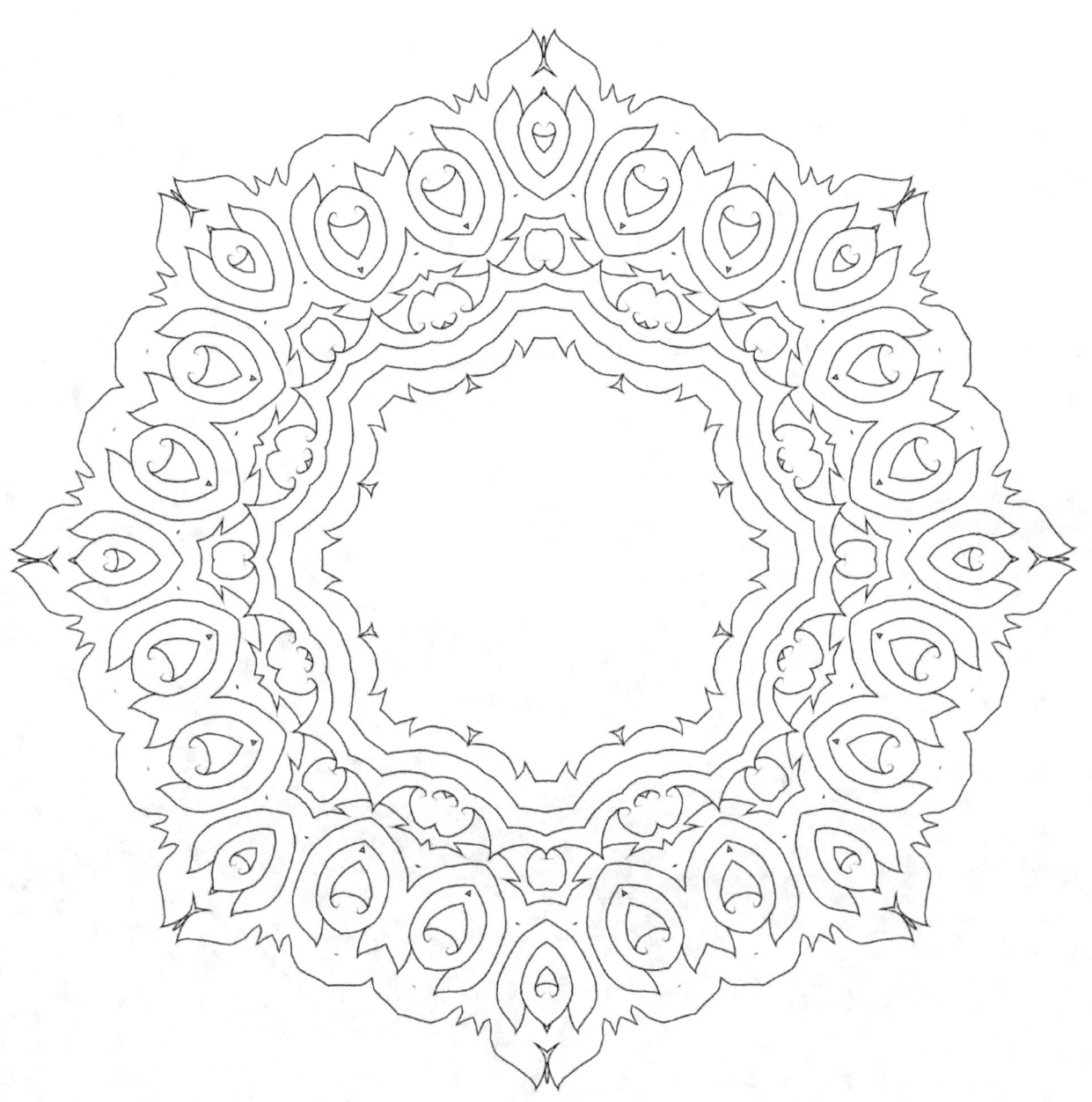

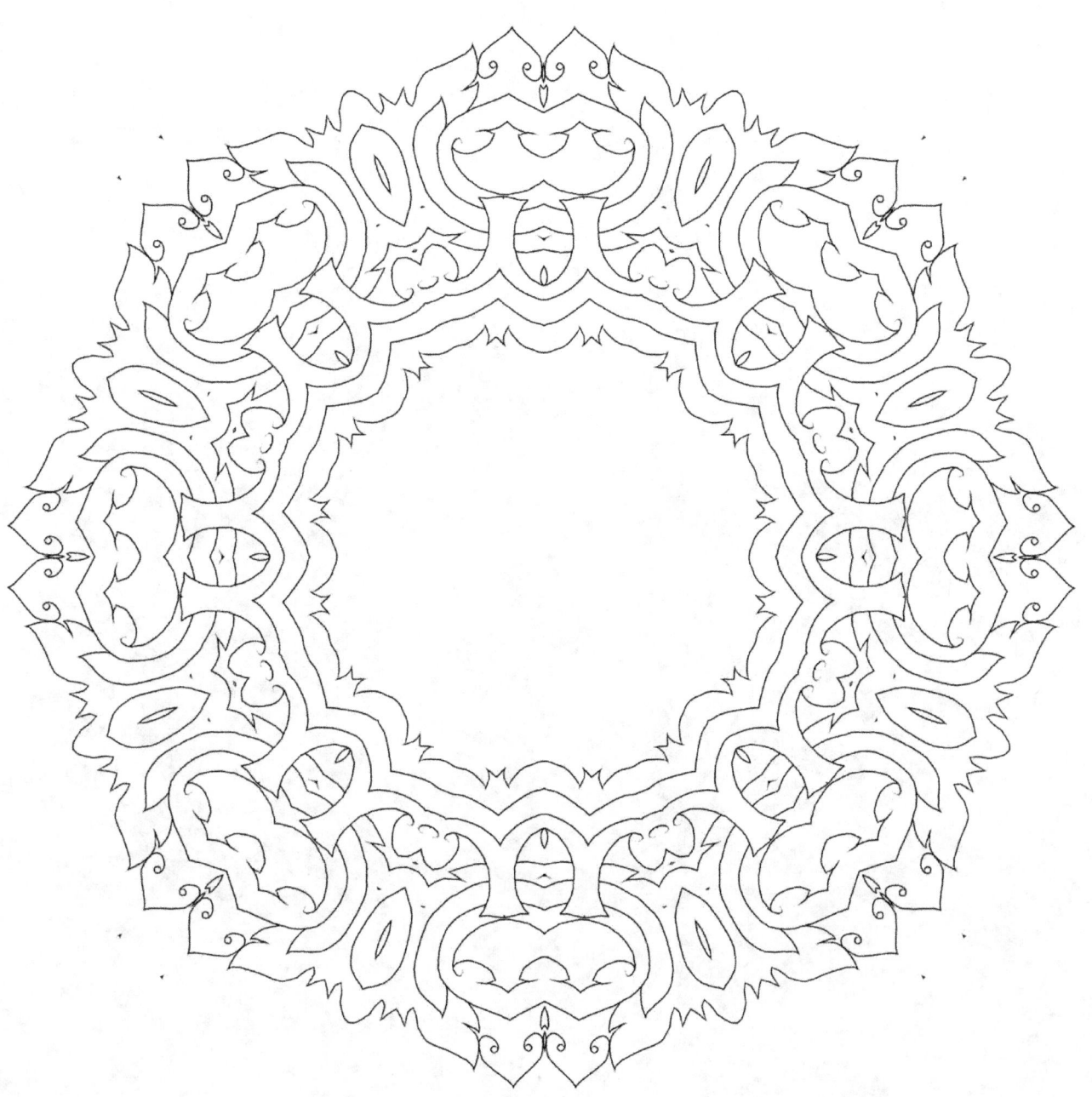

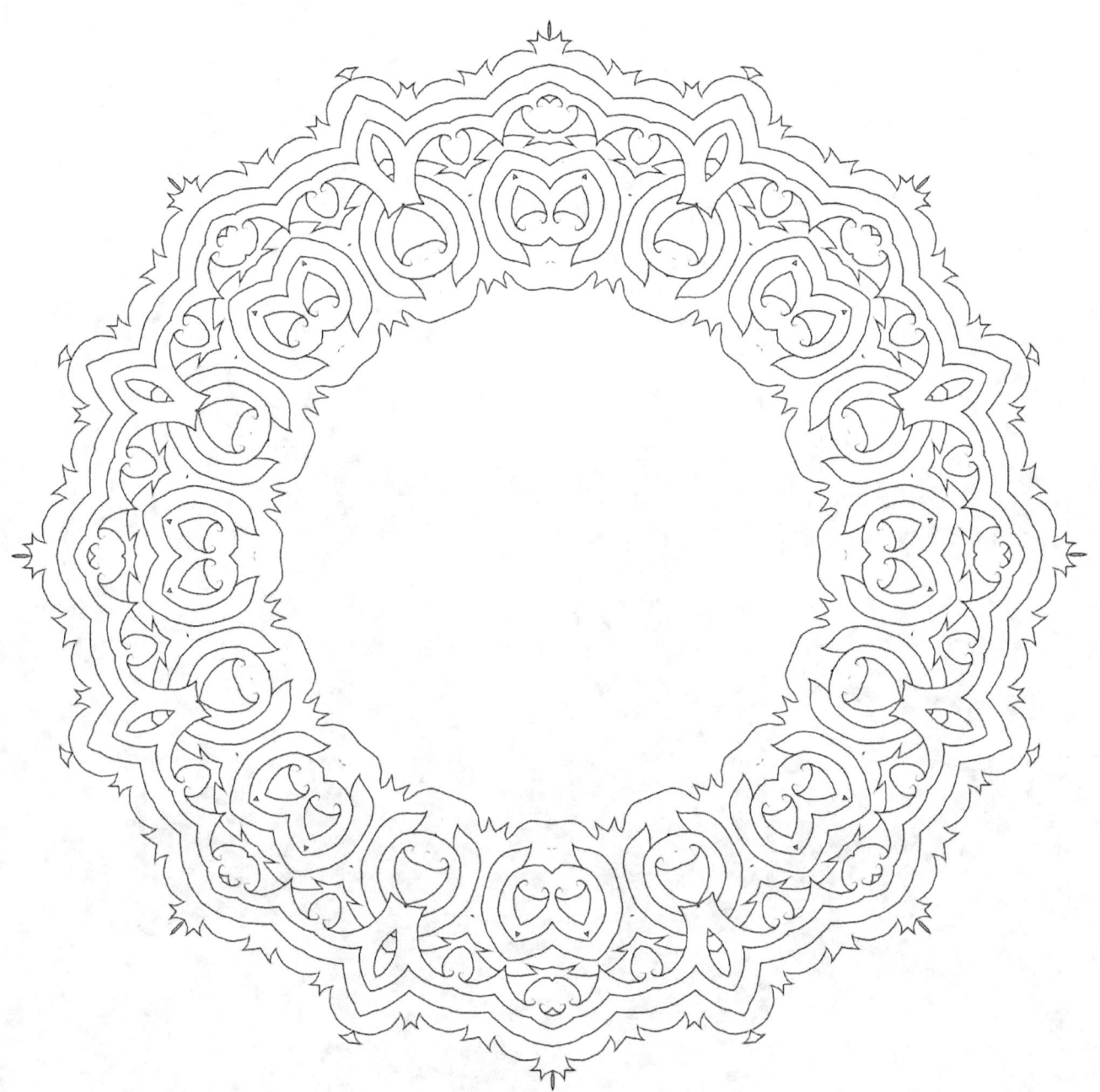

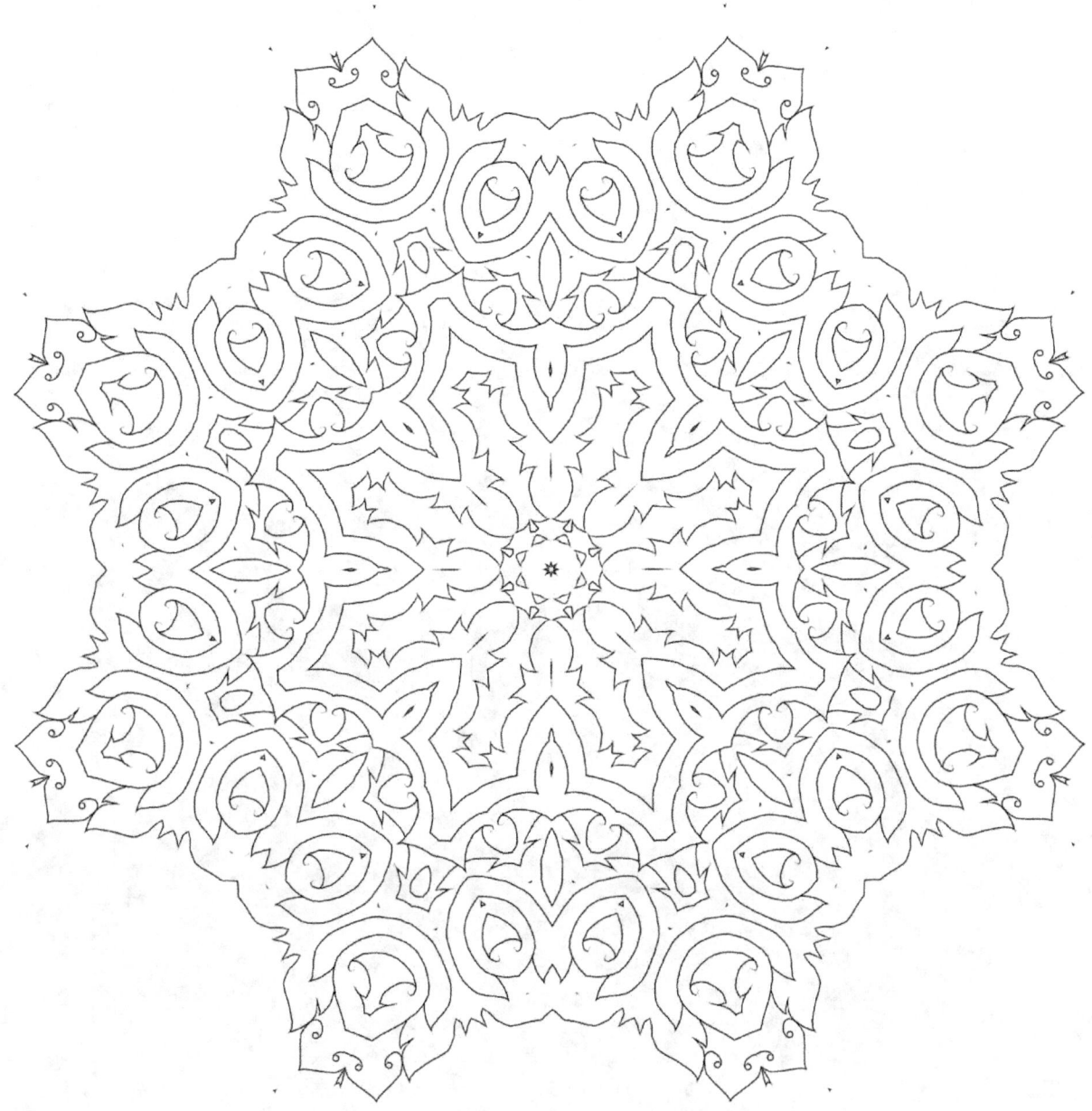

Thank you

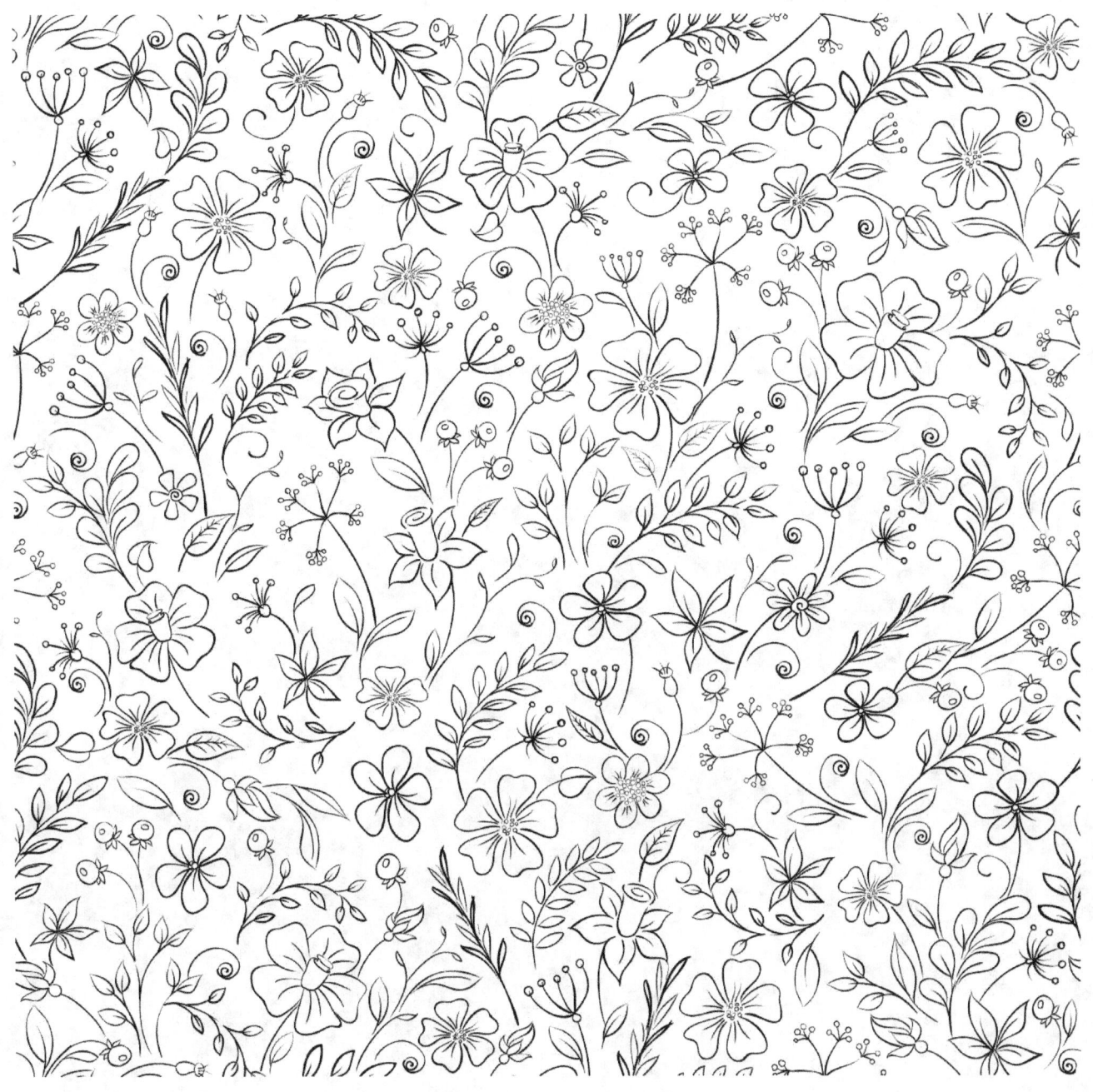

www.ingramcontent.com/pod-product-compliance
Lightning Source LLC
Chambersburg PA
CBHW081117180526
45170CB00008B/2885